best-loved Christmas carols, readings and poetry

best-loved Christmas carols, readings and poetry

Compiled by Martin Manser

Associate editor: David H. Pickering

Collins

This edition produced for Premier Direct Group Plc in 2005

Collins
an imprint of HarperCollins Publishers
77–85 Fulham Palace Road
London w6 8jb

www.collins.co.uk

First published in Great Britain in 2005 by
HarperCollins Publishers

10 9 8 7 6 5 4 3 2 1

Copyright © Martin Manser 2005
www.martinmanser.com

Martin Manser asserts the moral right to be
identified as the author of this work.

A catalogue record for this book is available from the British Library.

ISBN 0 00 776030 2

Typeset by Rowland Phototypesetting Ltd,
Bury St Edmunds, Suffolk
Printed and bound by Clays Ltd, St Ives plc

Unless otherwise specified, Scripture quotations are
taken from the New Revised Standard Version Bible,
copyright © 1989, by the National Council of the Churches
of Christ in the U.S.A., and are used by permission.

Contents

Introduction

Christmas: the very word conjures up a sense of celebration, excitement . . . and bustle. The Christmas season is a unique time of year, but the pressures of commercialism, the trappings associated with Christmas and the expectations we have of it all threaten to overshadow its real significance.

At the heart of Christmas is the most amazing fact: God took on our humanity and was born as a child in Bethlehem. This good news, reiterated in many different ways in this collection of carols, poems and readings, is meant to affect our lives the whole year round. So we have included material that explores the implications of Christmas, urging us to lead lives that reflect the message of peace on earth and goodwill to all.

This collection is designed both as a reference work and a resource for personal devotion. Each carol, reading or poem is given an introduction which provides interesting or helpful background information. All the readings are arranged in alphabetical order of title (ignoring 'A' or 'The' at the beginning of the title). For ease of reference there are also indexes at the beginning of the book to enable you to find a particular item by reference to its title and first line, its author, or, where appropriate, its Bible reference.

It has been a joy to edit this compilation, which we trust will take us back to the heart of the first Christmas, 'that to you is born . . . a Saviour, who is the Messiah, the Lord' (Luke 2:11). May we respond not only with our worship, praise and adoration but also with changed lives that actually live out the message of Christmas all through the year.

Martin H. Manser
David H. Pickering

Index of Titles and First Lines

Author Index

Byrom, John	Christians, awake!
Cappeau, Placide	O holy night
Caswall, Edward	See, amid the winter's snow
Cennick, John	Lo! He comes with clouds descending
Chesterton, G. K.	A Christmas carol
	The wise men
Collison, Valerie	Celebrations
Cummings, E. E.	little tree
de la Mare, Walter	Mistletoe
Dickens, Charles	A Christmas Carol
	The Pickwick Papers
Dix, William Chatterton	As with gladness men of old
	What child is this?
Earey, Mark	A Christingle song
Edgar, Marriott	Old Sam's Christmas pudding
Eliot, T. S.	Journey of the magi
Evelyn, John	A Puritan Christmas
Gerhardt, Paul	All my heart this night rejoices
Gifford, William	Rejoice, ye tenants of the earth
Heber, Reginald	Brightest and best of the sons of the morning
Hémy, H. F.	Angels we have heard on high
Hill, Richard	Now ys the time of Crystymas
Hopkins, John Henry	We three kings of Orient are
Hughes, Ted	Minstrel's song
Kipling, Rudyard	Christmas in India
Lewis, C. Day	The Christmas tree
Longfellow, Henry Wadsworth	Christmas bells
Luther, Martin	From heaven above to earth I come
MacDonald, Mary	Child in the manger
McGinley, Phyllis	All the days of Christmas
	Lady selecting her Christmas cards
MacNeice, Louis	Christmas shopping
May, Robert L.	Rudolph the red-nosed reindeer
Milne, A.A.	King John's Christmas
Milton, John	Hymn on the morning of Christ's nativity
Mohr, Joseph	Silent night
Montgomery, James	Angels, from the realms of glory
Moore, Clement C.	The night before Christmas
Neale, John Mason	Good King Wenceslas
Pepys, Samuel	A Pepysian Christmas
Perry, Michael	The Calypso carol
Pierpont, James Lord	Jingle bells
Prudentius, Aurelius Clemens	Of the Father's heart begotten
Rossetti, Christina	In the bleak mid-winter
	Love came down at Christmas
Sears, Edmund H.	It came upon a midnight clear
Shaw, George Bernard	A Shavian Christmas
Sims, George R.	Christmas Day in the workhouse
Swinburne, Algernon	Three damsels in the queen's chamber

Bible References

Genesis 3:8–15, 17–19	Adam and Eve in the garden
Numbers 24:15–19	Out of Jacob
2 Samuel 7:11–16	David's dynasty will last for ever
Isaiah 7:14–15	Behold a virgin shall conceive
Isaiah 9:2–7	For unto us a child is born
Isaiah 11:1–9	The rod of Jesse
Isaiah 40:1–11	The voice in the wilderness
Isaiah 49:1–18	A light to the nations
Daniel 7:13–14	To him was given dominion
Micah 4:1–7	Swords into ploughshares
Micah 5:2–5	Out of Bethlehem
Malachi 3:1–4	The messenger of God
Malachi 4:1–6	The sun of righteousness
Matthew 1:18–25	Joseph and Mary
Matthew 2:1–12	The three wise men
Matthew 2:13–18	The flight into Egypt
Luke 1:5–25	Zechariah and Elizabeth
Luke 1:26–38	The Annunciation
Luke 1:39–56	The Magnificat
Luke 1:67–79	Zechariah's song of thanksgiving
Luke 2:1–7	No room at the inn
Luke 2:8–20	The shepherds and the angels
Luke 2:25–38	Simeon and Anna
John 1:1–14	In the beginning was the Word
John 3:16–21	God so loved the world
John 14:1–13	I am the way
2 Corinthians 8:1–9	The grace of God
Galatians 4:4–6	When the fullness of time had come
Philippians 2:5–11	Jesus Christ is Lord
Colossians 1:15–23	The firstborn of all creation
1 Timothy 3:14–16	The mystery of our religion
Titus 2:11–3:8	Declare these things
Hebrews 1:1–2:4	God has spoken
1 John 1:1–14	The Word of life
1 John 4:7–21	God is love

Adam and Eve in the garden

This passage, from Genesis 3:8–15, 17–19, describes the result of humanity's disobedience. When Adam and Eve ate the forbidden fruit, the outcome was separation from God. The birth of Christ, and his death on the cross, has made a new relationship with God possible. These verses make up the first lesson of the traditional Service of Nine Lessons and Carols, which is broadcast from King's College, Cambridge each Christmas Eve.

They heard the sound of the LORD God walking in the garden at the time of the evening breeze, and the man and his wife hid themselves from the presence of the LORD God among the trees of the garden. But the LORD God called to the man, and said to him, 'Where are you?' He said, 'I heard the sound of you in the garden, and I was afraid, because I was naked; and I hid myself.' He said, 'Who told you that you were naked? Have you eaten from the tree of which I commanded you not to eat?' The man said, 'The woman whom you gave to be with me, she gave me fruit from the tree, and I ate.' Then the LORD God said to the woman, 'What is this that you have done?' The woman said, 'The serpent tricked me, and I ate.' The LORD God said to the serpent, 'Because you have done this, cursed are you among all animals and among all wild creatures; upon your belly you shall go, and dust you shall eat all the days of your life. I will put enmity between you and the woman, and between your offspring and hers; he will strike your head, and you will strike his heel.'

And to the man he said, 'Because you have listened to the voice of your wife, and have eaten of the tree about which I commanded "You shall not eat of it," cursed is the ground because of you; in toil you shall eat of it all the days of your life; thorns and thistles it shall bring forth for you; and you shall eat the plants of the field. By the sweat of your face you shall eat bread until you return to the ground, for out of it you were taken; you are dust, and to dust you shall return.'

Adam lay ybounden

This carol is a traditional choice for the Service of Nine Lessons and Carols at King's College, Cambridge and was originally included as a memorial to one of the chapel's directors of music, Boris Ord (1897–1961), who provided the musical setting. The carol remains Ord's only published composition. The carol was first recorded in a fifteenth-century manuscript, which also produced 'Lullay, my liking'.

Adam lay ybounden,
Bounden in a bond;
Four thousand winter
Thought he not too long.
All for an apple,
An apple that he took,
As clerkes finden
Written in their book.
Ne had the apple taken been,
The apple taken been,
Ne had never our Lady
Abeen heavene queen.
Blessed be the time
That apple taken was;
Therefore we moun singen:
Deo gracias! Deo gracias! Deo gracias!

Anonymous

All my heart this night rejoices

Paul Gerhardt wrote this carol as a hymn-writer and preacher in the German parish of Luebben. The uplifting tone of the carol is particularly poignant when considered in light of the events in Gerhardt's own life at the time – he had been expelled from his previous pastorate on political grounds and was still grieving the deaths of his wife and four of his five children.

All my heart this night rejoices
As I hear
Far and near
Sweetest angel voices,
'Christ is born,' Their choirs are singing
Till the air
Ev'rywhere
Now with joy is ringing.

Forth today the Conqueror goeth,
Who the foe,
Sin and woe,
Death and hell, o'erthroweth.
God is man, man to deliver;
His dear Son
Now is one
With our blood forever.

Shall we still dread God's displeasure,
Who, to save,
Freely gave
His most cherished Treasure?
To redeem us, he hath given
His own Son
From the throne
Of his might in heaven.

He becomes the Lamb that taketh
Sin away
And for aye
Full atonement maketh.

For our like his own he tenders;
And our race,
By his grace,
Meet for glory renders.

Hark! A voice from yonder manger,
Soft and sweet,
Doth entreat:
'Flee from woe and danger.
Brethren, from all ills that grieve you,
You are freed;
All you need
I will surely give you.'

Come, then, let us hasten yonder;
Here let all,
Great and small,
Kneel in awe and wonder.
Love him who with love is yearning;
Hail the star
That from far,
Bright with hope is burning.

Dearest Lord, thee will I cherish.
Though my breath
Fail in death,
Yet I shall not perish,
But with thee abide forever
There on high,
In that joy
Which can vanish never.

Paul Gerhardt (1607–76), translated by
Catherine Winkworth (1827–78)

All the days of Christmas

This poem by Phyllis McGinley, an American poet and writer for the New Yorker, *takes some of the features of the perennially-popular 'Twelve Days of Christmas' and weaves them into a meditation on family and love against the backdrop of the modern festive season.*

What shall my true love
Have from me
To pleasure his Christmas
Wealthily?
The partridge has flown
From our pear tree.

Flown with our summers,
Are the swans, the geese.
Milkmaids and drummers
Would leave him little peace.
I've no gold ring
And no turtle dove.
So what can I bring
To my true love?

A coat for the drizzle,
Chosen at the store;
A saw and a chisel
For mending the door;
A pair of red slippers
To slip on his feet;
Three striped neckties;
Something sweet.

He shall have all
I can best afford –
No pipers, piping,
No leaping lord,
But a fine fat hen
For his Christmas board;
Two pretty daughters
(Versed in the role)

To be worn like pinks
In his buttonhole;
And the tree of my heart
With its calling linnet,
My evergreen heart
And the bright bird in it.

Phyllis McGinley (1905–78)

Angels, from the realms of glory

James Montgomery was born into a peasant family in Ayrshire and, having abandoned his studies for the ministry, pursued a career as a poet. He became the author of over 400 hymns and carols. These lines first appeared in The Sheffield Iris, a journal for which Montgomery was editor, on Christmas Eve 1816. They are usually sung to the tune of the French 'Les anges dans nos campagnes', which is also used for another familiar carol, 'Angels we have heard on high'.

Angels, from the realms of glory,
Wing your flight o'er all the earth;
Ye who sang Creation's story
Now proclaim Messiah's birth!
Come and worship Christ the new-born King!
Come and worship, worship Christ the new-born King!

Shepherds, in the field abiding,
Watching o'er your flocks by night:
God with man is now residing,
Yonder shines the Infant Light.
Come and worship Christ the new-born King!
Come and worship, worship Christ the new-born King!

Sages, leave your contemplations:
Brighter visions beam afar.
Seek the Great Desire of Nations:
Ye have seen his natal star.
Come and worship Christ the new-born King!
Come and worship, worship Christ the new-born King!

Saints, before the altar bending,
Watching long in hope and fear:
Suddenly the Lord, descending,
In his temple shall appear.
Come and worship Christ the new-born King!
Come and worship, worship Christ the new-born King!

Though an infant now we view him,
He shall fill his Father's throne,
Gather all the nations to him;
Every knee shall then bow down.
Come and worship Christ the new-born King!
Come and worship, worship Christ the new-born King!

James Montgomery (1771–1854)

Angels we have heard on high

This carol is French in origin, having been translated from the French 'Les anges dans nos campagnes' by Bishop James Chadwick and first published in 1860. By then it was already an established favourite in France and Quebec. Tradition has it that in the second century Pope Telesphorus ordained that all the faithful should sing the words 'Gloria in excelsis Deo' at Christmas, hence its inclusion as a refrain here.

Angels we have heard on high,
Singing sweetly o'er the plains,
And the mountains in reply
Echoing their joyous strains:
Gloria in excelsis Deo!

Shepherds, why this jubilee?
Why these joyous strains prolong?
What the gladsome tidings be
Which inspire your heavenly song?
Gloria in excelsis Deo!

Come to Bethlehem and see
Him whose birth the angels sing;
Come, adore on bended knee
Christ the Lord, the new-born King!
Gloria in excelsis Deo!

See him in a manger laid,
Whom the choirs of angels praise;
Mary, Joseph, lend your aid,
While our hearts in love we raise.
Gloria in excelsis Deo!

H. F. Hémy (1818–88), after James Chadwick (1813–82)

The Annunciation

This passage, from Luke 1:26–38, relates how Mary receives a visit from an angel and hears the news that she is to become the mother of Christ. As part of the background to the story of Christ's birth, it is recited in churches throughout Christendom as an integral part of carol services.

In the sixth month the angel Gabriel was sent by God to a town in Galilee called Nazareth, to a virgin engaged to a man whose name was Joseph, of the house of David. The virgin's name was Mary. And he came to her and said, 'Greetings, favoured one! The Lord is with you.' But she was much perplexed by his words and pondered what sort of greeting this might be. The angel said to her, 'Do not be afraid, Mary, for you have found favour with God. And now, you will conceive in your womb and bear a son, and you will name him Jesus. He will be great, and will be called the Son of the Most High, and the Lord God will give to him the throne of his ancestor David. He will reign over the house of Jacob for ever, and of his kingdom there will be no end.' Mary said to the angel, 'How can this be, since I am a virgin?' The angel said to her, 'The Holy Spirit will come upon you, and the power of the Most High will overshadow you; therefore the child to be born will be holy; he will be called Son of God. And now, your relative Elizabeth in her old age has also conceived a son; and this is the sixth month for her who was said to be barren. For nothing will be impossible with God.' Then Mary said, 'Here am I, the servant of the Lord; let it be with me according to your word.' Then the angel departed from her.

As with gladness men of old

William Chatterton Dix worked in shipping insurance in Bristol, but also wrote hymns in his spare time. He wrote this popular Epiphany hymn (the most successful of his compositions), on 6 January 1860, when he was in his early twenties), after illness prevented him attending his local Anglican church. He was inspired by the Gospel lesson for the day, the Epiphany story as told at Matthew 2:1–12. The tune to which the hymn is sung was composed by the German composer Conrad Kocher and is commonly called 'Dix', although Dix himself professed to dislike the tune.

As with gladness men of old
Did the guiding star behold;
As with joy they hailed its light,
Leading onward, beaming bright;
So, most gracious God, may we
Evermore be led to thee.

As with joyful steps they sped
To that lowly manger bed,
There to bend the knee before
Him whom heaven and earth adore;
So may we with willing feet
Ever seek thy mercy seat.

As they offered gifts most rare
At that manger rude and bare;
So may we with holy joy,
Pure and free from sin's alloy,
All our costliest treasures bring,
Christ, to thee, our heavenly King.

Holy Jesus, every day
Keep us in the narrow way;
And, when earthly things are past,
Bring our ransomed souls at last
Where they need no star to guide,
Where no clouds thy glory hide.

In the heavenly country bright
Need they no created light;
Thou its light, its joy, its crown,
Thou its sun which goes not down;
There for ever may we sing
Alleluias to our King.

William Chatterton Dix (1837–98)

Away in a manger

The authorship of this hugely popular Christmas carol is often credited,
mistakenly, to Martin Luther, probably because it was first published in a
Lutheran hymnal early in the nineteenth century. In fact, the author is
unknown, although the third verse is known to have been the work of John
Thomas McFarland (1851–1913). The carol is thought to have been first
performed by American Lutherans in 1883 during celebrations of the 400th
anniversary of Luther's birth. It is sung in the UK to a tune by William
J. Kirkpatrick (1838–1921), but in the USA to a tune by James R. Murray
(c.1841–1905).

Away in a manger, no crib for a bed,
The little Lord Jesus laid down his sweet head;
The stars in the bright sky looked down where he lay
The little Lord Jesus, asleep on the hay.

The cattle are lowing, the Baby awakes,
But little Lord Jesus, no crying he makes.
I love thee, Lord Jesus! Look down from the sky,
And stay by my cradle till morning is nigh.

Be near me, Lord Jesus: I ask thee to stay
Close by me for ever, and love me, I pray;
Bless all the dear children in thy tender care,
And take us to heaven to live with thee there.

Anonymous

Behold a virgin shall conceive

This brief passage, from Isaiah 7:14–15, looks forward to the birth of Christ in the years to come. It gives details of a virgin who would give birth to a son. His name would be 'Immanuel', which means 'God with us' (Matthew 1:23).

Therefore the Lord himself will give you a sign. Look, the young woman is with child and shall bear a son, and shall name him Immanuel. He shall eat curds and honey by the time he knows how to refuse the evil and choose the good.

The boar's head carol

This old English carol is traditionally sung as the main dish (a wild boar's head) is brought in during the Christmas feast at Queen's College, Oxford. It has remained in use, sung to a tune written as late as 1901, despite the fact that wild boars became extinct in England by the end of the seventeenth century.

The boar's head in hand bear I,
Bedecked with bays and rosemary;
And I pray you my masters be merry,
Quot estis in convivio.

Caput apri defero
Reddens laudes Domino.

The boar's head, as I understand,
Is the bravest dish in all the land
When thus bedecked with a gay garland;
Let us servire cantico.

Our steward hath provided this
In honour of the King of Bliss,
Which on this day to be served is
In Reginensi Atrio.

Anonymous

Brightest and best of the sons of the morning

This carol was written by Reginald Heber, the Anglican vicar of the small Shropshire village of Hodnet, on Epiphany Sunday, 1811. His inspiration was Matthew 2:1–12, the Gospel reading for that particular day. The carol became widely popular, being taken up with particular enthusiasm by Methodists, Baptists and Presbyterians. Heber went on to serve as Bishop of Calcutta, where he eventually died. His other compositions include the hymn 'Holy, holy, holy'.

Hail the blest morn! See the great Mediator
Down from the regions of glory descend!
Shepherds, go worship the Babe in the manger!
Lo! For his guard the bright angels attend.

Brightest and best of the sons of the morning,
Dawn on our darkness and lend us thine aid;
Star in the East, the horizon adorning,
Guide where our infant Redeemer was laid!

Cold on his cradle the dewdrops are shining,
Low lies his bed with the beasts of the stall;
Angels adore him, in slumber reclining,
Wise men and shepherds before him do fall.

Say, shall we yield him, in costly devotion,
Odours of Edom and off'rings divine,
Gems from the mountain and pearls from the ocean,
Myrrh from the forest and gold from the mine?

Vainly we offer each ample oblation,
Vainly with gold would his favour secure;
Richer by far is the heart's adoration,
Dearer to God are the prayers of the poor.

Reginald Heber (1783–1826)

The Calypso carol

This song, with its catchy tune, is one of the more popular of relatively recently introduced Christmas songs. It invites a fresh response to Jesus Christ as Saviour.

See Him lying on a bed of straw,
A draughty stable with an open door;
Mary cradling the babe she bore –
The prince of glory is His name.

O now carry me to Bethlehem
To see the Lord of love again:
Just as poor as was the stable then,
The prince of glory when He came!

Star of silver, sweep across the skies,
Show where Jesus in the manger lies;
Shepherds, swiftly from your stupor rise
To see the saviour of the world!

Angels sing again the song you sang,
Sing the glory of God's gracious plan;
Sing that Bethlehem's little baby can
Be the saviour of us all.

Mine are riches, from your poverty,
From your innocence, eternity;
Mine forgiveness by your death for me,
Child of sorrow for my joy.

Michael Perry (1942–96)

Words: Michael Perry © Mrs B Perry/Jubilate Hymns
Used by permission

Celebrations

This Christmas song is a popular contemporary carol and a frequent choice for children and families to sing during the festive season.

Come and join the celebration.
It's a very special day.
Come share our jubilation:
There's a new King born today!

See the Shepherds
Hurry down to Bethlehem,
Gaze in wonder
At the Son of God
Who lay before them.

Wise men journey,
Led to worship by a star,
Kneel in homage,
Bringing precious gifts
From lands afar.

'God is with us,'
Round the world the message bring.
He is with us.
'Welcome!' all the bells
On earth are peeling.

> *Valerie Collison (b.1933)*

Permission has been sought.

Child in the manger

This carol recalls the simplicity of the Christmas message: that God became a human being and lived among us. He has taken away our sin and redeemed us. He is worthy of our worship, praise and adoration.

Child in the manger,
infant of Mary;
outcast and stranger,
Lord of all:
child who inherits
all our transgressions,
all our demerits
on him fall.

Once the most holy
child of salvation
gentle and lowly
lived below;
now as our glorious
mighty Redeemer,
see him victorious
over each foe.

Prophets foretold him,
infant of wonder;
angels behold him
on his throne;
worthy our Saviour
of all their praises;
happy for ever
are his own.

Mary Macdonald (1789–1872)
translated by I. Macbean (1853–1931)

Christians, awake!

John Byrom, a scholar of Trinity College, Cambridge, wrote this popular Christmas hymn in 1749 in response to a request from his young daughter, Dolly, for an unusual Christmas present. She was delighted when she came down to breakfast on Christmas Day that year to find a scroll bearing the poem at her place. The lines were subsequently set to music by John Wainwright (c.1723–68), the organist at Stockport Parish Church, who directed the choir that sang it outside Byrom's house on Christmas morning 1750.

Christians, awake! Salute the happy morn
Whereon the Saviour of the World was born!
Rise to adore the mystery of love,
Which hosts of angels chanted from above;
With them the joyful tidings first begun
Of God incarnate and the Virgin's Son.

Unto the watchful shepherds it was told,
Who heard the angelic herald's voice: 'Behold!
I bring good tidings of a Saviour's birth
To you and all the nations of the earth:
This day hath God fulfilled his promised word,
This day is born a Saviour, Christ the Lord!

'In David's city, shepherds, ye shall find
The long-foretold Redeemer of mankind;
Joseph and Mary, in a stable there,
Guard the sole object of the Almighty's care;
Wrapped up in swaddling-clothes, the Babe divine
Lies in a manger: this shall be your sign.'

He spake, and straightway the celestial choir
In hymns of joy, unknown before, conspire.
The praises of redeeming love they sung,
And heaven's whole orb with Hallelujahs rung;
God's highest glory was their anthem still,
Peace on the earth, and mutual good will.

To Bethlehem straight the enlightened shepherds ran
To see the wonder God hath wrought for man,
And found, with Joseph and the blessed Maid,
Her Son, the Saviour, in a manger laid:
To human eyes none present but they two,
Where heaven was pointing its concentred view.

Amazed, the wondrous story they proclaim,
The first apostles of his infant fame;
While Mary keeps and ponders in her heart
The heavenly vision which the swains impart,
They to their flocks, still praising God, return,
And their glad hearts within their bosoms burn.

Let us, like these good shepherds, then, employ
Our grateful voices to proclaim the joy;
Like Mary, let us ponder in our mind
God's wondrous love in saving lost mankind:
Artless and watchful as these favoured swains,
While virgin meekness in our heart remains.

Trace we the Babe, who has retrieved our loss,
From his poor manger to his bitter Cross,
Treading his steps, assisted by his grace,
Till man's first heavenly state again takes place,
And, in fulfilment of the Father's will,
The place of Satan's fallen host we fill.

Then may we hope, the angelic thrones among,
To sing, redeemed, a glad triumphal song.
He that was born upon this joyful day
Around us all his glory shall display;
Save by his love, incessant we shall sing
Of angels and of angel-men the King.

John Byrom (1692–1763)

A Christingle song

'Christingle' means 'Christ light' and is a symbol of the Christian faith. The Christingle orange represents the world, the red ribbon around it signifies the blood of Christ, the fruits symbolise the fruits of the earth in their four seasons and the candle represents Jesus, the light of the world. This song may be sung to the tune 'Give me oil in my lamp (Sing Hosanna)'.

The Christingle begins with an orange,
telling us of the world God made.
By the fruits of the earth in their seasons,
we can see the love of God displayed.

> *Sing Christingle! Sing Christingle!*
> *Sing Christingle, it's the light of Christ.*
> *Sing Christingle! Sing Christingle!*
> *Sing Christingle, light of Christ.*

God of love, we give thanks now for Jesus;
we remember his birth again.
But the red ribbon round the Christingle
tells the story of his cross and pain.

To complete the Christingle: a candle,
shining out in the darkest night.
Jesus promised to lead us and guide us;
come and celebrate the world's true light!

Mark Earey (b.1965)

Christmas

*This poem by John Betjeman contrasts the frivolities of the modern Christmas
with the serious message of Christ's birth.*

The bells of waiting Advent ring,
The Tortoise stove is lit again
And lamp-oil light across the night
Has caught the streaks of winter rain
In many a stained-glass window sheen
From Crimson Lake to Hooker's Green.

The holly in the windy hedge
And round the Manor House the yew
Will soon be stripped to deck the ledge,
The altar, font and arch and pew,
So that the villagers can say
'The church looks nice' on Christmas Day.

Provincial public houses blaze
And Corporation tramcars clang,
On lighted tenements I gaze
Where paper decorations hang,
And bunting in the red Town Hall
Says 'Merry Christmas to you all'.

And London shops on Christmas Eve
Are strung with silver bells and flowers
As hurrying clerks the City leave
To pigeon-haunted classic towers,
And marbled clouds go scudding by
The many-steepled London sky.

And girls in slacks remember Dad,
And oafish louts remember Mum,
And sleepless children's hearts are glad,
And Christmas-morning bells say 'Come!'
Even to shining ones who dwell
Safe in the Dorchester Hotel.

And is it true? And is it true,
This most tremendous tale of all,
Seen in a stained-glass window's hue,
A Baby in an ox's stall?
The Maker of the stars and sea
Become a Child on earth for me?

And is it true? For if it is,
No loving fingers tying strings
Around those tissued fripperies,
The sweet and silly Christmas things,
Bath salts and inexpensive scent
And hideous tie so kindly meant,

No love that in a family dwells,
No carolling in frosty air,
Nor all the steeple-shaking bells
Can with this single Truth compare –
That God was Man in Palestine
And lives to-day in Bread and Wine.

John Betjeman (1906–84)

Reproduced by permission of John Murray Publishers

Christmas bells

In this poem, the festivities of Christmas Day are contrasted with the grim realities of life. Longfellow penned this plea for peace on Christmas Day 1863, at a time when America was convulsed by civil war, just six months after the Battle of Gettysburg.

I heard the bells on Christmas Day
Their old, familiar carols play,
And wild and sweet
The words repeat
Of peace on earth, good will to men!

I thought how, as the day had come,
The belfries of all Christendom
Had rolled along
The unbroken song
Of peace on earth, good will to men!

And in despair I bowed my head:
'There is no peace on earth,' I said,
'For hate is strong
And mocks the song
Of peace on earth, good will to men!'

Then pealed the bells more loud and deep:
'God is not dead; nor doth he sleep!
The wrong shall fail,
The right prevail,
With peace on earth, good will to men!'

Henry Wadsworth Longfellow (1824–84)

A Christmas carol

This is a poem of simple adoration that often appears in anthologies of best-loved Christmas verse.

The Christ-child lay on Mary's lap,
His hair was like a light.
(O weary, weary were the world,
But here is all aright.)

The Christ-child lay on Mary's breast,
His hair was like a star.
(O stern and cunning are the kings,
But here the true hearts are.)

The Christ-child lay on Mary's heart,
His hair was like a fire.
(O weary, weary is the world,
But here the world's desire.)

The Christ-child stood at Mary's knee,
His hair was like a crown.
And all the flowers looked up at him,
And all the stars looked down.

G. K. Chesterton (1874–1936)

A Christmas Carol

This extract from the Charles Dickens short story, 'A Christmas Carol', is hugely loved and exemplifies the popular notion of a traditional Victorian Christmas family meal, not least the anxiety of the cook that all should turn out as planned. Tiny Tim's Christmas blessing is often quoted during the festive season.

His active little crutch was heard upon the floor, and back came Tiny Tim before another word was spoken, escorted by his brother and sister to his stool before the fire; and while Bob, turning up his cuffs – as if, poor fellow, they were capable of being made more shabby – compounded some hot mixture in a jug with gin and lemons, and stirred it round and round and put it on the hob to simmer; Master Peter, and the two ubiquitous young Cratchits went to fetch the goose, with which they soon returned in high procession.

Such a bustle ensued that you might have thought a goose the rarest of all birds; a feathered phenomenon, to which a black swan was a matter of course – and in truth it was something very like it in that house. Mrs Cratchit made the gravy (ready beforehand in a little saucepan) hissing hot; Master Peter mashed the potatoes with incredible vigour; Miss Belinda sweetened up the apple-sauce; Martha dusted the hot plates; Bob took Tiny Tim beside him in a tiny corner at the table; the two young Cratchits set chairs for everybody, not forgetting themselves, and mounting guard upon their posts, crammed spoons in their mouths, lest they should shriek for goose before their turn came to be helped. At last the dishes were set on, and grace was said. It was succeeded by a breathless pause, as Mrs Cratchit, looking slowly all along the carving-knife, prepared to plunge it in the breast, but when she did, and when the long-expected gush of stuffing issued forth, one murmur of delight arose all round the board, and even Tiny Tim, excited by the two young Cratchits, beat on the table with the handle of his knife, and feebly cried Hurrah!

There never was such a goose. Bob said he didn't believe there ever was such a goose cooked. Its tenderness and flavour, size and cheapness, were the themes of universal admiration. Eked out by apple-sauce and mashed potatoes, it was a sufficient dinner for the whole family; indeed, as Mrs Cratchit said with great delight (surveying one small atom of a bone upon the dish), they hadn't ate it all at last! Yet every one had had enough, and the youngest Cratchits in particular, were steeped in sage and onion to the eyebrows! But now, the plates being changed by Miss Belinda, Mrs Cratchit left the room alone – too nervous to bear witness – to take the pudding up and bring it in.

Suppose it should not be done enough! Suppose it should break in turning out! Suppose somebody should have got over the wall of the back-yard, and stolen it, while they were merry with the goose – a supposition at which the two young Cratchits became livid! All sorts of horrors were supposed.

Hallo! A great deal of steam! The pudding was out of the copper. A smell like a washing-day! That was the cloth. A smell like an eating-house and a pastrycook's next door to each other, with a laundress's next door to that! That was the pudding! In half a minute, Mrs Cratchit entered – flushed, but smiling proudly – with the pudding, like a speckled cannon-ball, so hard and firm, blazing in half of half-a-quartern of ignited brandy, and bedight with Christmas holly stuck into the top.

Oh, a wonderful pudding! Bob Cratchit said, and calmly too, that he regarded it as the greatest success achieved by Mrs Cratchit since their marriage. Mrs Cratchit said that now the weight was off her mind, she would confess she had had her doubts about the quantity of flour. Everybody had something to say about it, but nobody said or thought it was at all a small pudding for a large family. It would have been flat heresy to do so. Any Cratchit would have flushed to hint at such a thing.

At last the dinner was all done, the cloth was cleared, the hearth swept, and the fire made up. The compound in the jug being tasted, and considered perfect, apples and oranges were put upon the table, and a shovel-full of chestnuts on the fire. Then all the Cratchit family drew round the hearth, in what Bob Cratchit called a circle, meaning half a one; and at Bob Cratchit's elbow stood the family display of glass. Two tumblers, and a custard-cup without a handle.

These held the hot stuff from the jug, however, as well as golden goblets would have done; and Bob served it out with beaming looks, while the chestnuts on the fire sputtered and cracked noisily. Then Bob proposed:

'A Merry Christmas to all, my dears. God bless us!'

Which all the family re-echoed.

'God bless us every one!' said Tiny Tim, the last of all.

Charles Dickens (1812–70)

Christmas Day in the workhouse

This melodramatic monologue ranked among the most popular pieces regularly recited on Victorian music hall stages. It was the work of George R. Sims, a social reformer and criminologist as well as a playwright. The monologue was guaranteed to send a chill down the spines of its original audiences, and even today it may serve as a salutary reminder of the lot of those less fortunate. After World War I it was often parodied, most successfully by comedian Billy Bennett as 'Christmas Day in the cookhouse'.

It is Christmas Day in the workhouse,
And the cold bare walls are bright
With garlands of green and holly,
And the place is a pleasant sight:
For with clean-washed hands and faces,
In a long and hungry line
The paupers sit at the tables,
For this is the hour they dine.

And the guardians and their ladies,
Although the wind is east,
Have come in their furs and wrappers,
To watch their charges feast;
To smile and be condescending,
Put pudding on pauper plates,
To be hosts at the workhouse banquet
They've paid for – with the rates.

Oh, the paupers are meek and lowly
With their 'Thank'ee kindly, mum's';
So long as they fill their stomachs,
What matter it whence it comes?
But one of the old men mutters,
And pushes his plate aside:
'Great God!' he cries, 'but it chokes me!
For this is the day *she* died.'

The guardians gazed in horror,
The master's face went white;
'Did a pauper refuse their pudding?'
'Could their ears believe aright?'
Then the ladies clutched their husbands,
Thinking the man would die,
Struck by a bolt, or something,
By the outraged One on high.

But the pauper sat for a moment,
Then rose 'mid a silence grim,
For the others had ceased to chatter,
And trembled in every limb.
He looked at the guardians' ladies,
Then, eyeing their lords, he said,
'I eat not the food of villains
Whose hands are foul and red:

'Whose victims cry for vengeance
From their dank, unhallowed graves.'
'He's drunk!' said the workhouse master.
'Or else he's mad, and raves.'
'Not drunk or mad,' cried the pauper,
'But only a hunted beast,
Who, torn by the hounds and mangled,
Declines the vulture's feast.

'I care not a curse for the guardians,
And I won't be dragged away.
Just let me have the fit out,
It's only on Christmas Day
That the black past comes to goad me,
And prey on my burning brain;
I'll tell you the rest in a whisper –
I swear I won't shout again.

'Keep your hands off me, curse you!
Hear me right out to the end.
You come here to see how paupers
The season of Christmas spend.

You come here to watch us feeding,
As they watch the captured beast.
Hear why a penniless pauper
Spits on your paltry feast.

'Do you think I will take your bounty,
And let you smile and think
You're doing a noble action
With the parish's meat and drink?
Where is my wife, you traitors –
The poor old wife you slew?
Yes, by the God above us,
My Nance was killed by you!

'Last winter my wife lay dying,
Starved in a filthy den;
I had never been to the parish –
I came to the parish then.
I swallowed my pride in coming,
For, ere the ruin came,
I held up my head as a trader,
And I bore a spotless name.

'I came to the parish, craving
Bread for a starving wife,
Bread for the woman who'd loved me
Through fifty years of life;
And what do you think they told me,
Mocking my awful grief?
That "the House" was open to us,
But they wouldn't give "out relief".

'I slunk to the filthy alley –
'Twas a cold, raw Christmas eve –
And the bakers' shops were open,
Tempting a man to thieve;
But I clenched my fists together,
Holding my head awry,
So I came to her empty-handed,
And mournfully told her why.

'Then I told her "the House" was open;
She had heard of the ways of *that*,
For her bloodless cheeks went crimson,
And up in her rags she sat,
Crying, "Bide the Christmas here, John,
We've never had one apart;
I think I can bear the hunger –
The other would break my heart."

'All through that eve I watched her,
Holding her hand in mine,
Praying the Lord, and weeping
Till my lips were salt as brine.
I asked her once if she hungered,
And as she answered "No,"
The moon shone in at the window
Set in a wreath of snow.

'Then the room was bathed in glory,
And I saw in my darling's eyes
The far-away look of wonder
That comes when the spirit flies;
And her lips were parched and parted,
And her reason came and went,
For she raved of our home in Devon,
Where our happiest years were spent.

'And the accents, long forgotten,
Came back to the tongue once more,
For she talked like the country lassie
I woo'd by the Devon shore.
Then she rose to her feet and trembled,
And fell on the rags and moaned,
And, "Give me a crust – I'm famished –
For the love of God!" she groaned.

'I rushed from the room like a madman,
And flew to the workhouse gate,
Crying, "Food for a dying woman!"
And the answer came, "Too late".
They drove me away with curses;

Then I fought with a dog in the street,
And tore from the mongrel's clutches
A crust he was trying to eat.

'Back, through the filthy by-lanes!
Back, through the trampled slush!
Up to the crazy garret,
Wrapped in an awful hush.
My heart sank down at the threshold,
And I paused with a sudden thrill,
For there in the silv'ry moonlight
My Nance lay, cold and still.

'Up to the blackened ceiling
The sunken eyes were cast –
I knew on those lips all bloodless
My name had been the last;
She'd called for her absent husband –
O God! Had I but known! –
Had called in vain, and in anguish
Had died in that den – *alone.*

'Yes, there, in a land of plenty,
Lay a loving woman dead,
Cruelly starved and murdered
For a loaf of the parish bread.
At yonder gate, last Christmas,
I craved for a human life.
You, who would feast us paupers,
What of my murdered wife!

'There, get ye gone to your dinners;
Don't mind me in the least;
Think of the happy paupers
Eating your Christmas feast;
And when you recount their blessings
In your smug parochial way,
Say what you did for *me*, too,
Only last Christmas Day.'

   George R. Sims (1847–1922)

Christmas in India

In this poem Rudyard Kipling gives voice to those for whom Christmas has a bitter taste; in this case, the soldiers of the Raj serving far from their native land in a country much removed from the traditional Yuletide comforts.

Dim dawn behind the tamarisks – the sky is saffron-yellow –
As the women in the village grind the corn,
And the parrots seek the river-side, each calling to his fellow
That the Day, the staring Eastern Day, is born.
O the white dust on the highway! O the stenches in the byway!
O the clammy fog that hovers over earth!
And at Home they're making merry 'neath the white and scarlet
    berry –
What part have India's exiles in their mirth?

Full day behind the tamarisks – the sky is blue and staring –
As the cattle crawl afield beneath the yoke,
And they bear One o'er the field-path, who is past all hope or caring,
To the ghat below the curling wreaths of smoke.
Call on Rama, going slowly, as ye bear a brother lowly –
Call on Rama – he may hear, perhaps, your voice!
With our hymn-books and our psalters we appeal to other altars,
And to-day we bid 'good Christian men rejoice!'

High noon behind the tamarisks – the sun is hot above us –
As at Home the Christmas Day is breaking wan.
They will drink our healths at dinner – those who tell us how they love
    us,
And forget us till another year be gone!
O the toil that knows no breaking! O the *Heimweh*, ceaseless, aching!
O the black dividing Sea and alien Plain!
Youth was cheap – wherefore we sold it. Gold was good – we hoped to
    hold it.
And to-day we know the fullness of our gain!

Grey dusk behind the tamarisks – the parrots fly together –
As the Sun is sinking slowly over Home;
And his last ray seems to mock us shackled in a lifelong tether
That drags us back howe'er so far we roam.
Hard her service, poor her payment – she in ancient, tattered
    raiment –
India, she the grim Stepmother of our kind.
If a year of life be lent her, if her temple's shrine we enter,
The door is shut – we may not look behind.

Black night behind the tamarisks – the owls begin their chorus –
As the conches from the temple scream and bray.
With the fruitless years behind us and the hopeless years before us,
Let us honour, O my brothers, Christmas Day!
Call a truce, then, to our labours – let us feast with friends and
    neighbours,
And be merry as the custom of our caste;
For, if 'faint and forced the laughter,' and if sadness follow after,
We are richer by one mocking Christmas past.

Rudyard Kipling (1865–1936)

*Reproduced with permission of A P Watt Ltd, on behalf of
The National Trust for Places of Historic Interst or Natural Beauty.*

Christmas is coming, the geese are getting fat

This universal Christmas ditty urging the giving of alms at Yuletide is by an anonymous hand, but is sometimes attributed to 'Mother Goose', the mythical fount of many children's rhymes and stories.

Christmas is coming, the geese are getting fat,
Please to put a penny in the old man's hat;
If you haven't got a penny, a ha'penny will do,
If you haven't got a ha'penny,
God bless you.

> *Anonymous*

Ch

In t   sents a panoramic view of a contemporary
Chr   for sale to Christmas shoppers may have
cha   d by these and other festive rituals remain
as r   as first written.

Spe   on gifts for Christmas –
Swi   and draperied jungles –
Wha   ands and sons
Diff

Foxe   d the plate glass –
Scre   s of paper –
Only   lates are free
From

Some   pes in the flesh,
Lightly manoeuvres the crowd, trilling with laughter;
After a couple of years her feet and her brain will
Tire like the others.

The great windows marshal their troops for assault on the purse
Something-and-eleven the yard, hoodwinking logic,
The eleventh hour draining the gurgling pennies
Down to the conduits,

Down to the sewers of money – rats and marshgas –
Bubbling in maundering music under the pavement;
Here go the hours of routine, the weight on our eyelids –
Pennies on corpses'.

While over the street in the centrally heated public
Library dwindling figures with sloping shoulders
And hands in pockets, weighted in the boots like chessmen,
Stare at the printed

Columns of ads, the quickest road to riches,
Starting at a little and temporary but once we're

Started who knows whether we shan't continue,
Salaries rising,

Rising like a salmon against the bullnecked river,
Bound for the spawning-ground of care-free days –
Good for a fling before the golden wheels run
Down to a standstill.

And Christ is born – the nursery glad with baubles,
Alive with light and washable paint and children's
Eyes, expects as its due the accidental
Loot of a system.

Smell of the South – oranges in silver paper,
Dates and ginger, the benison of firelight,
The blue flames dancing round the brandied raisins,
Smiles from above them,

Hands from above them as of gods but really
These their parents, always seen from below, them-
Selves are always anxious looking across the
Fence to the future –

Out there lies the future gathering quickly
Its blank momentum; through the tubes of London
The dead winds blow the crowds like beasts in flight from
Fire in the forest.

The little fir trees palpitate with candles
In hundreds of chattering households where the suburb
Straggles like nervous handwriting, the margin
Blotted with smokestacks.

Further out on the coast the lighthouse moves its
Arms of light through the fog that wads our welfare,
Moves its arms like a giant at Swedish drill whose
Mind is a vacuum.

Louis MacNeice (1907–63)

Permission has been sought.

A Christmas song

Nicholas Breton was the author of a wide range of satirical, religious, romantic and political poems. In this piece the author congratulates himself for having evaded the usual distractions of the festive season, but the reader is left to speculate whether the underlying tone is one of satisfaction or regret.

The Christmas now is past, and I have kept my fast,
With prayer every day;
And, like a country clown, with nodding up and down,
Have passed the time away.

As for old Christmas games, or dancing with fine dames,
Or shows or pretty plays;
A solemn oath I swear, I came not where they were,
Not all these holy-days.

I did not sing one note, except it were by rote,
Still buzzing like a bee;
To ease my heavy heart of some though little smart,
For want of other glee.

And as for pleasant wine, there was no drink so fine,
For to be tasted here;
Full simple was my fare, if that I should compare,
The same to Christmas Cheer.

I saw no kind of sight that might my mind delight,
Believe me, noble dame.
But everything I saw did fret at woe my maw,
To think upon the same.

Upon some bushy balk full fain I was to walk,
In woods, from tree to tree,
For want of better room; but since my fatal doom
Hath so appointed me;

I stood therewith content, the Christmas full was spent,
In hope that God will send
A better yet next year, my heavy heart to cheer;
And so I make an end.

Nicholas Breton (c.1555–1626)

The Christmas tree

In this poem, C. Day Lewis celebrates the Christmas tree's role as the chief decoration in countless homes during the festive season. To him, the Christmas tree is at once a symbol of transient life and of eternal mystery.

Put out the lights now!
Look at the Tree, the rough tree dazzled
In oriole plumes of flame,
Tinselled with twinkling frost fire, tasselled
With stars and moons – the same
That yesterday hid in the spinney and had no fame
Till we put out the lights now.

Hard are the nights now:
The fields at moonrise turn to agate,
Shadows are cold as jet;
In dyke and furrow, in copse and faggot
The frost's tooth is set;
And stars are the sparks whirled out by the north wind's fret
On the flinty nights now.

So feast your eyes now
On mimic star and moon-cold bauble:
Worlds may wither unseen
But the Christmas Tree is a tree of fable,
A phoenix in evergreen,
And the world cannot change or chill what its mysteries mean
To your hearts and eyes now.

The vision dies now
Candle by candle; the tree that embraced it
Returns to its own kind,
To be earthed again and weather as best it
May the frost and the wind.
Children, it too had its hour – you will not mind
If it lives or dies now.

C. Day Lewis (1898–1963)

*From the Complete Poems by C Day Lewis published by Sinclair-Stevenson (1992) ©
1992 in this edition the Estate of C Day Lewis. Reprinted by permission of The Random
House Group Ltd.*

Come, Thou long-expected Jesus

This advent carol ranks among the most popular of the 4,000 or more hymns and carols penned by Charles Wesley. Based on Haggai 2:7 ('And I will shake all the nations, so that the treasure of all nations shall come, and I will fill this house with splendour'), it was first published in 1744.

Come, Thou long-expected Jesus,
Born to set Thy people free;
From our fears and sins release us;
Let us find our rest in Thee.
Israel's strength and consolation,
Hope of all earth Thou art;
Dear desire of every nation,
Joy of every longing heart.

Born Thy people to deliver,
Born a child, and yet a king,
Born to reign in us forever,
Now Thy gracious kingdom bring.
By Thine own eternal spirit
Rule in our hearts alone;
By Thine all-sufficient merit
Raise use to Thy glorious throne.

Charles Wesley (1707–88)

The Coventry carol

The lines for this celebrated carol were written by an unknown hand around the fourteenth century. They formed part of the Pageant of the Shearmen and Tailors, one of the famous Coventry mystery plays performed on the feast of Corpus Christi, and sung by the mothers of the children of Bethlehem just before their children are put to death on the orders of King Herod. The tradition is that the women sang lullabies in the futile hope of preventing their children from making a noise and thus being discovered by Herod's soldiers. The accuracy of the lines as we now have them has been challenged since the only original manuscript was lost in a fire in 1879.

Lully, lulla, thou little tyne child,
By, by, lully, lulla, thou little tyne child,
By, by, lully, lullay.

O sisters too,
How may we do
For to preserve this day
This pore yongling
For whom we do sing:
'By, by, lully, lullay'?

Herod the King
In his raging
Chargid he hath this day
His men of might
In his owne sight
All yonge children to slay.

That wo is me,
Pore child, for thee,
And ever morne and say
For thi parting
Nether say nor singe:
'By, by, lully, lullay.'

Anonymous

David's dynasty will last for ever

This passage, from 2 Samuel 7:11–16, underlines the fact that God will build David a house – a royal dynasty – that will last for ever. However, it also warns that when God's people are disobedient and fall into sin they will be punished. In the case of David himself, although he was largely faithful to God, his sin with Bathsheba was followed by the death of his first child with her, but God's promises continued to be fulfilled as their son Solomon succeeded David as king.

Moreover, the LORD declares to you that the LORD will make you a house. When your days are fulfilled and you lie down with your ancestors, I will raise up your offspring after you, who shall come forth from your body, and I will establish his kingdom. He shall build a house for my name, and I will establish the throne of his kingdom for ever. I will be a father to him, and he shall be a son to me. When he commits iniquity, I will punish him with a rod such as mortals use, with blows inflicted by human beings. But I will not take my steadfast love from him, as I took it from Saul, whom I put away from before you. Your house and your kingdom shall be made sure for ever before me; your throne shall be established for ever.

Deck the halls with boughs of holly

Originally a Welsh song, this carol stems from the canu penillion *tradition of singers taking turns to extemporise their own lines to the tune played by a harpist, each making way for the next when their own invention flagged. Each line is followed by an answering* 'Fa la la la la la la la la' *chorus sung by all present.*

Deck the halls with boughs of holly:
'Tis the season to be jolly!
Don we now our gay apparel,
Troll the ancient Yuletide carol.

See the blazing Yule before us
Strike the harp and join the chorus!
Follow me in merry measure,
While I tell of Yuletide treasure.

Fast away the old year passes,
Hail the new, ye lads and lasses!
Sing we, joyous, all together
Heedless of the wind and weather.

Anonymous

Declare these things

These lines, from Titus 2:11–3:8, offer guidance on living a virtuous Christian life based on the model of Christ himself. Our lives should be lived in response to the generous and self-giving love of Christ. Those who follow Jesus Christ are called upon to lead godly, pure and obedient lives, looking forward to his return.

For the grace of God has appeared, bringing salvation to all, training us to renounce impiety and worldly passions, and in the present age to live lives that are self-controlled, upright, and godly, while we wait for the blessed hope and the manifestation of the glory of our great God and Saviour, Jesus Christ. He it is who gave himself for us that he might redeem us from all iniquity and purify for himself a people of his own who are zealous for good deeds.

Declare these things; exhort and reprove with all authority. Let no one look down on you. Remind them to be subject to rulers and authorities, to be obedient, to be ready for every good work, to speak evil of no one, to avoid quarrelling, to be gentle, and to show every courtesy to everyone. For we ourselves were once foolish, disobedient, led astray, slaves to various passions and pleasures, passing our days in malice and envy, despicable, hating one another. But when the goodness and loving-kindness of God our Saviour appeared, he saved us, not because of any works of righteousness that we had done, but according to his mercy, through the water of rebirth and renewal by the Holy Spirit. This Spirit he poured out on us richly through Jesus Christ our Saviour, so that, having been justified by his grace, we might become heirs according to the hope of eternal life. The saying is sure.

I desire that you insist on these things, so that those who have come to believe in God may be careful to devote themselves to good works; these things are excellent and profitable to everyone.

Ding! dong! merrily on high

This old carol is sung to a tune written in the sixteenth century by Thoinot Arbeau (1520–95). Thoinot Arbeau is actually a pseudonym for Jehan Tabourot, the real name of a French cleric who in 1588 published a treatise on dancing entitled Orchésographie. *The original tune was called 'Branle de l'official' and had a distinctly dubious reputation, being performed to a rather scandalous dance in which men lifted their female partners into the air.*

Ding! dong! merrily on high
In heav'n the bells are ringing.
Ding! Dong! verily the sky
Is riv'n with angels singing.
Gloria! Hosanna in excelsis!

E'en so here below, below,
Let steeple bells be swungen,
And 'Io, io, io!'
By priest and people sungen.

Pray you dutifully prime
Your matin chime, ye ringers!
May you beautifully rime
Your evetime song, ye singers!

    G. R. Woodward (1848–1934)

Everywhere, everywhere, Christmas tonight!

Phillips Brooks was an American clergyman who eventually rose to the post of Episcopal Bishop of Massachusetts and is usually remembered as the author of the ever-popular carol 'O little town of Bethlehem'. This simple poem, speaking of the universality of Christmas, ranks among his better-known lesser writings.

Everywhere, everywhere, Christmas tonight!
Christmas in lands of the fir-tree and pine,
Christmas in lands of the palm-tree and vine,
Christmas where snow peaks stand solemn and white,
Christmas where cornfields stand sunny and bright,
Christmas where children are hopeful and gay,
Christmas where old men are patient and grey,
Christmas where peace, like a dove in his flight,
Broods o'er brave men in the thick of the fight;
Everywhere, everywhere, Christmas tonight!

For the Christ-child who comes is the master of all;
No palace too great, no cottage too small.

Phillips Brooks (1835–93)

The first Nowell

This is a traditional English carol of unknown authorship. It was included in William Sandys's West Country collection Christmas Carols Ancient and Modern *(1833) and the modern musical arrangement was contributed by John Stainer (1840–1901) in 1871.*

The first 'Nowell!' the angel did say,
Was to certain poor shepherds in fields as they lay;
In fields where they lay keeping their sheep,
On a cold winter's night that was so deep.
Nowell! nowell! nowell! nowell!
Born is the King of Israel.

They looked up and saw a star,
Shining in the east, beyond them far,
And to the earth, it gave great light,
And so it continued both day and night.

And by the light of that same star
Three wise men came from country far;
To seek for a King was their intent,
And to follow the star wheresoever it went.

This star drew nigh to the north-west:
O'er Bethlehem it took its rest;
And there it did both stop and stay,
Right over the place where Jesus lay.

Then did they know assuredly
Within that house the King did lie;
One entered in then for to see,
And found the Babe in poverty.

Then entered in those wise men three,
Fell reverently, upon their knee,
And offered there, in his presence,
Both gold and myrrh, and frankincense.

Between an ox-stall and an ass
This Child there truly borned was;
For want of clothing they did him lay
All in the manger, among the hay.

Then let us all with one accord
Sing praises to our heavenly Lord
That hath made heaven and earth of nought,
And with his blood mankind hath bought.

If we in our lifetime shall do well
We shall be free from death and hell,
For God hath prepared for us all
A resting-place in general.

Anonymous

The first-born of all creation

This biblical passage, from Colossians 1:15–23, states the supremacy of Christ over all creation. He existed before the world was made and yet lived as a man in order to bring humanity back to God. At Christmas we focus on his birth as a baby, but it is his teaching and then his death on the cross that gives the Christmas story its full significance.

He is the image of the invisible God, the firstborn of all creation; for in him all things in heaven and on earth were created, things visible and invisible, whether thrones or dominions or rulers or powers – all things have been created through him and for him. He himself is before all things, and in him all things hold together. He is the head of the body, the church; he is the beginning, the firstborn from the dead, so that he might come to have first place in everything. For in him all the fullness of God was pleased to dwell, and through him God was pleased to reconcile to himself all things, whether on earth or in heaven, by making peace through the blood of his cross.

And you who were once estranged and hostile in mind, doing evil deeds, he has now reconciled in his fleshly body through death, so as to present you holy and blameless and irreproachable before him – provided that you continue securely established and steadfast in the faith, without shifting from the hope promised by the gospel that you heard, which has been proclaimed to every creature under heaven.

The flight into Egypt

This passage, from Matthew 2:13–18, describes what came to be known as the 'Massacre of the Innocents'. It is often recited on 28 December, the Feast of the Innocents, commemorating the event.

Now after they had left, an angel of the Lord appeared to Joseph in a dream and said, 'Get up, take the child and his mother, and flee to Egypt, and remain there until I tell you; for Herod is about to search for the child, to destroy him.' Then Joseph got up, took the child and his mother by night, and went to Egypt, and remained there until the death of Herod. This was to fulfil what had been spoken by the Lord through the prophet, 'Out of Egypt I have called my son.'

When Herod saw that he had been tricked by the wise men, he was infuriated, and he sent and killed all the children in and around Bethlehem who were two years old or under, according to the time that he had learned from the wise men. Then was fulfilled what had been spoken through the prophet Jeremiah:

'A voice was heard in Ramah,
wailing and loud lamentation,
Rachel weeping for her children;
she refused to be consoled, because they are no more.'

For unto us a child is born

This passage, from Isaiah 9:2–7, is often read at Christmas. It is particularly well known from its repetition by the composer George Frideric Handel in the celebrated 'Hallelujah Chorus' from his oratorio Messiah *(1742). Handel himself once recalled how he had been inspired to write his masterpiece: 'I saw the Heavens opened, and the Great white God sitting on the Throne . . . whether I was in my body or out of my body as I wrote it I know not. God knows.'*

The people who walked in darkness have seen a great light; those who lived in a land of deep darkness – on them light has shined.

You have multiplied the nation, you have increased its joy; they rejoice before you as with joy at the harvest, as people exult when dividing plunder.

For the yoke of their burden, and the bar across their shoulders, the rod of their oppressor, you have broken as on the day of Midian.

For all the boots of the tramping warriors and all the garments rolled in blood shall be burned as fuel for the fire.

For a child has been born for us, a son given to us; authority rests upon his shoulders; and he is named Wonderful Counsellor, Mighty God, Everlasting Father, Prince of Peace.

His authority shall grow continually, and there shall be endless peace for the throne of David and his kingdom. He will establish and uphold it with justice and with righteousness from this time onwards and for evermore.

The zeal of the LORD of hosts will do this.

The friendly beasts

This traditional English carol, describing how the animals brought gifts to the infant Christ, is thought to have been written in the twelfth century.

Jesus, our brother, kind and good,
Was humbly born in a stable rude;
And the friendly beasts around Him stood.
Jesus, our brother, kind and good.

'I,' said the Donkey, shaggy and brown,
'I carried His mother up hill and down;
I carried His mother to Bethlehem town.'
'I,' said the Donkey, shaggy and brown.

'I,' said the Cow, all white and red,
'I gave Him my manger for His bed;
I gave Him my hay to pillow His head.'
'I,' said the Cow, all white and red.

'I,' said the Sheep, with the curly horn,
'I gave Him my wool for His blanket warm;
He wore my coat on Christmas morn.'
'I,' said the Sheep, with the curly horn.

'I,' said the Dove, from the rafters high,
'I cooed Him to sleep that He should not cry;
We cooed Him to sleep, my mate and I.'
'I,' said the Dove, from the rafters high.

Thus every beast by some glad spell,
In the stable dark was glad to tell
Of the gift he gave Emmanuel,
The gift he gave Emmanuel.

Anonymous

From heaven above to earth I come

This carol is relatively unknown in English-speaking countries, but is one of the most popular of all carols elsewhere in the world. Also known by its German title 'Vom Himmel hoch da komm ich her', it is recognised as one of the carols written by Martin Luther. It is thought he wrote it for a Christmas Eve service in which his son, Hans, was due to participate, the opening verses being spoken by an actor playing an angel and the rest by children.

From heaven above to earth I come,
To bear good news to every home;
Glad tidings of great joy I bring,
Whereof I now will say and sing,

'To you this night is born a Child
Of Mary, chosen mother mild;
This little Child of lowly birth,
Shall be the joy of all your earth.

'"Tis Christ our God, who far on high
Hath heard your sad and bitter cry
Himself will your salvation be;
Himself from sin will make you free.'

Welcome to earth, Thou noble Guest,
Through whom even wicked men are blest!
Thou com'st to share our misery;
What can we render, Lord, to Thee?

Were earth a thousand times as fair,
Beset with gold and jewels rare,
She yet were far too poor to be
A narrow cradle, Lord, for Thee.

Ah! Dearest Jesus, Holy Child,
Make Thee a bed, soft, undefiled,
Within my heart, that it may be
A quiet chamber kept for Thee.

My heart for very joy doth leap;
My lips no more can silence keep;
I too must raise with joyful tongue
That sweetest ancient cradle song,

'Glory to God in highest heaven,
Who unto man His Son hath given!
While angels sing with pious mirth
A glad New Year to all on earth.'

Martin Luther (1483–1546), translated by
Catherine Winkworth (1827–78)

A frosty Christmas Eve

This atmospheric poem, prompted by the ringing of church bells on Christmas Eve, conjures up the magic unique to this one night of the year.

A frosty Christmas Eve when the stars were shining
Fared I forth alone where westward falls the hill
And from many a village in the water'd valley
Distant music reached me peals of bells a-ringing:
The constellated sounds ran sprinkling on earth's floor
As the dark vault above with stars was spangled o'er.

Then sped my thought to keep that first Christmas of all
When the shepherds watching by their folds ere the dawn
Heard music in the fields and marvelling could not tell
Whether it were angels or the bright stars singing.

Now blessed be the towers that crown England so fair
That stand up strong in prayer unto God for our souls:
Blessed be their founders (said I) and our country-folk
Who are ringing for Christ in the belfries to-night
With arms lifted to clutch the rattling ropes that race
Into the dark above and the mad romping din.

But to me heard afar it was heav'nly music
Angels' song comforting as the comfort of Christ
When he spake tenderly to his sorrowful flock:
The old words came to me by the riches of time
Mellow'd and transfigured as I stood on the hill
Hark'ning in the aspect of th' eternal silence.

Robert Bridges (1844–1930)

Gaudete!

These verses appeared in the Finnish Piae Cantiones *in 1582, though without music. They have their origins in a medieval Bohemian song entitled 'Ezechielis porta' and were sung to an old Czech Christmas tune. It is thought the song was picked up by Finnish students in Prague.*

Gaudete! gaudete! Christus est natus
Ex Maria Virgine: gaudete!

Tempus adest gratiae,
Hoc quod optabamus;
Carmina laeticiae
Devote reddamus.

Deus homo factus est,
Natura mirante;
Mundus renovatus est
A Christo regnante.

Ezechielis porta
Clausa pertransitur;
Unde Lux est orta,
Salus invenitur.

Ergo nostra concio
Psallat jam in lustro;
Benedicat Domino:
Salus Regi nostro.

Anonymous

Go tell it on the mountain

This Christmas song began life as a traditional American folk song, sung by black slaves on the plantations. It was published in Religious Songs of the Negro as sung on the Plantations, *edited by Thomas P. Fenner, in 1909.*

In the time of David,
Some call him a king,
And if a child is true-born,
Lord Jesus will hear him sing:
Go tell it on the mountain,
Over the hills and everywhere;
Go tell it on the mountain
That Jesus Christ is born!

When I was a seeker
I sought both night and day;
I ask the Lord to help me,
And he show me the way.

He made me a watchman
Upon a city wall,
And if I am a Christian
I am the least of all.

Anonymous

God has spoken

This passage, found at Hebrews 1:1–2:4, declares that in these last days God has revealed himself supremely through his Son, Jesus Christ, who is 'the exact imprint of God's very being' and superior to the angels. The reading ends with a warning to heed this teaching and to not neglect this great salvation.

Long ago God spoke to our ancestors in many and various ways by the prophets, but in these last days he has spoken to us by a Son, whom he appointed heir of all things, through whom he also created the worlds. He is the reflection of God's glory and the exact imprint of God's very being, and he sustains all things by his powerful word. When he had made purification for sins, he sat down at the right hand of the Majesty on high, having become as much superior to angels as the name he has inherited is more excellent than theirs.

For to which of the angels did God ever say, 'You are my Son; today I have begotten you'? Or again, 'I will be his Father, and he will be my Son'? And again, when he brings the firstborn into the world, he says, 'Let all God's angels worship him.'

Of the angels he says, 'He makes his angels winds, and his servants flames of fire.' But of the Son he says, 'Your throne, O God, is for ever and ever, and the righteous sceptre is the sceptre of your kingdom. You have loved righteousness and hated wickedness; therefore God, your God, has anointed you with the oil of gladness beyond your companions.'

And, 'In the beginning, Lord, you founded the earth, and the heavens are the work of your hands; they will perish, but you remain; they will all wear out like clothing; like a cloak you will roll them up, and like clothing they will be changed. But you are the same, and your years will never end.'

But to which of the angels has he ever said, 'Sit at my right hand until I make your enemies a footstool for your feet'? Are not all angels spirits in the divine service, sent to serve for the sake of those who are to inherit salvation?

Therefore we must pay greater attention to what we have heard, so that we do not drift away from it. For if the message declared through angels was valid, and every transgression or disobedience received a just penalty, how can we escape if we neglect so great a salvation? It was declared at first through the Lord, and it was attested to us by those who heard him, while God added his testimony by signs and wonders and various miracles, and by gifts of the Holy Spirit, distributed according to his will.

God is love

This celebrated passage, from 1 John 4:7–21, encapsulates the belief that love is the keystone of Christian faith. It is a message that is thought especially suitable at Christmas and this passage, which stresses the importance of close family relationships, is often chosen as a reading in churches during the festive period.

Beloved, let us love one another, because love is from God; everyone who loves is born of God and knows God. Whoever does not love does not know God, for God is love. God's love was revealed among us in this way: God sent his only Son into the world so that we might live through him. In this is love, not that we loved God but that he loved us and sent his Son to be the atoning sacrifice for our sins. Beloved, since God loved us so much, we also ought to love one another. No one has ever seen God; if we love one another, God lives in us, and his love is perfected in us.

By this we know that we abide in him and he in us, because he has given us of his Spirit. And we have seen and do testify that the Father has sent his Son as the Saviour of the world. God abides in those who confess that Jesus is the Son of God, and they abide in God. So we have known and believe the love that God has for us.

God is love, and those who abide in love abide in God, and God abides in them. Love has been perfected among us in this: that we may have boldness on the day of judgement, because as he is, so are we in this world. There is no fear in love, but perfect love casts out fear; for fear has to do with punishment, and whoever fears has not reached perfection in love. We love because he first loved us. Those who say, 'I love God', and hate their brothers or sisters, are liars; for those who do not love a brother or sister whom they have seen, cannot love God whom they have not seen. The commandment we have from him is this: those who love God must love their brothers and sisters also.

God rest ye merry, gentlemen

This is a traditional English carol from the West Country. It is one of the most familiar of all Christmas songs and even features in the short story A Christmas Carol *by Charles Dickens. Its acceptance in churches is, however, a relatively recent phenomenon. The tune to which these lines are usually sung was probably of French origin and may be heard in many other parts of Europe.*

God rest ye merry, gentlemen,
Let nothing you dismay,
For Jesus Christ, our Saviour,
Was born upon this day
To save us all from Satan's power
When we were gone astray.
O tidings of comfort and joy, comfort and joy,
O tidings of comfort and joy!

In Bethlehem in Jewry
This blessed Babe was born,
And laid within a manger
Upon this blessed morn;
The which his mother Mary
Nothing did take in scorn.

From God our heavenly Father
A blessed angel came,
And unto certain shepherds
Brought tidings of the same,
How that in Bethlehem was born
The Son of God by name.

'Fear not,' then said the angel,
'Let nothing you affright;
This day is born a Saviour
Of virtue, power and might,
So frequently to vanquish all
The friends of Satan quite.'

The shepherds at those tidings
Rejoiced much in mind,
And left their flocks a-feeding
In tempest, storm and wind,
And went to Bethlehem straightway
This blessed Babe to find.

But when to Bethlehem they came,
Whereat this Infant lay,
They found him in a manger
Where oxen feed on hay;
His mother Mary, kneeling,
Unto the Lord did pray.

Now to the Lord sing praises,
All you within this place,
And with true love and brotherhood
Each other now embrace.
The holy tide of Christmas
All others doth efface.

Anonymous

God so loved the world

These words, from John 3:16–21, reflect upon the purpose of Christ's coming: God loved the world so much that he sent his Son to give eternal life to all those who believe in him. The response called for is to turn from darkness to light and to trust in Jesus Christ.

For God so loved the world that he gave his only Son, so that everyone who believes in him may not perish but may have eternal life.

Indeed, God did not send the Son into the world to condemn the world, but in order that the world might be saved through him. Those who believe in him are not condemned; but those who do not believe are condemned already, because they have not believed in the name of the only Son of God. And this is the judgement, that the light has come into the world, and people loved darkness rather than light because their deeds were evil. For all who do evil hate the light and do not come to the light, so that their deeds may not be exposed. But those who do what is true come to the light, so that it may be clearly seen that their deeds have been done in God.

Good Christian friends, rejoice

This carol was included in the Piae Cantiones *(1582) and was probably of German origin. It is sometimes ascribed to a German Dominican monk called Heinrich Suso (1300–65), who in 1328 is said to have had a vision of angels dancing and singing the carol. The song may, however, have already been in existence before that time. The musical setting was contributed by J. S. Bach (1685–1750).*

Good Christian friends, rejoice
With heart and soul and voice!
Give ye heed to what we say:
News! News!
Jesus Christ is born today!
Ox and ass before him bow,
And he is in the manger now:
Christ is born today! Christ is born today!

Good Christian friends, rejoice
With heart and soul and voice!
Now ye hear of endless bliss:
Joy! Joy!
Jesus Christ was born for this!
He hath oped the heavenly door,
And man is blessed evermore:
Christ was born for this!

Good Christian friends, rejoice
With heart and soul and voice!
Now ye need not fear the grave:
Peace! Peace!
Jesus Christ was born to save!
Calls you one and calls you all,
To gain his everlasting hall:
Christ was born to save!

Anonymous, adapted by John Mason Neale (1818–66)

Good King Wenceslas

The historical Wenceslas was Vaclav the Good, and ruled Bohemia for seven years between 922 and his premature death at the age of 22 in 929. The incident described in this popular carol is not believed to have any basis in historical fact, though Vaclav was revered for his pious lifestyle and is remembered for such good deeds as the abolition of torture and the gallows. His charity ultimately proved his undoing, as his reforms threatened the wealth of the nobility: he was murdered while staying at his brother's castle, being put to death as he entered the church there. He is venerated today as the patron saint of the Czech Republic. St Stephen's Day (or Boxing Day) is a traditional date for showing charity towards the poor.

Good King Wenceslas looked out
On the feast of Stephen,
When the snow lay round about,
Deep and crisp and even;
Brightly shone the moon that night,
Though the frost was cruel,
When a poor man came in sight,
Gath'ring winter fuel.

'Hither, page, and stand by me;
If thou know'st it, telling –
Yonder peasant, who is he?
Where and what his dwelling?'
'Sire, he lives a good league hence,
Underneath the mountain,
Right against the forest fence,
By Saint Agnes' fountain.'

'Bring me flesh, and bring me wine!
Bring me pine logs hither!
Thou and I will see him dine
When we bear them thither.'
Page and monarch forth they went,
Forth they went together,
Through the rude wind's loud lament
And the bitter weather.

'Sire, the night is darker now,
And the wind blows stronger;
Fails my heart, I know not how,
I can go no longer.'
'Mark my footsteps, good my page,
Tread thou in them boldly:
Thou shalt find the winter's rage
Freeze thy blood less coldly.'

In his master's steps he trod,
Where the snow lay dinted;
Heat was in the very sod
Which the saint had printed.
Therefore, Christian men, be sure,
Wealth or rank possessing,
Ye who now will bless the poor
Shall yourselves find blessing.

John Mason Neale (1818–66)

The grace of God

This passage, from 2 Corinthians 8:1–9, praises the generosity of the churches of Macedonia towards their fellow believers in Jerusalem and in so doing celebrates the underlying value of giving, both at Christmas and at other times of the year. The supreme motivation for true Christian generosity is the example of Jesus Christ, who set aside his glory and submitted to the humiliation of becoming a man.

We want you to know, brothers and sisters, about the grace of God that has been granted to the churches of Macedonia; for during a severe ordeal of affliction, their abundant joy and their extreme poverty have overflowed in a wealth of generosity on their part. For, as I can testify, they voluntarily gave according to their means, and even beyond their means, begging us earnestly for the privilege of sharing in this ministry to the saints – and this, not merely as we expected; they gave themselves first to the Lord and, by the will of God, to us, so that we might urge Titus that, as he had already made a beginning, so he should also complete this generous undertaking among you. Now as you excel in everything – in faith, in speech, in knowledge, in utmost eagerness, and in our love for you – so we want you to excel also in this generous undertaking.

I do not say this as a command, but I am testing the genuineness of your love against the earnestness of others. For you know the generous act of our Lord Jesus Christ, that though he was rich, yet for your sakes he became poor, so that by his poverty you might become rich.

Hark! the herald angels sing

This carol (although changed in minor details from the original) is among the most celebrated of all the compositions of the great hymn writer Charles Wesley, founder, with his brother John, of the Methodist Church. It was written in 1739, just one year after Wesley's conversion to Christianity. The rousing tune to which the carol is sung today was the work of the composer Felix Mendelssohn (1809–47), written to commemorate the 400th anniversary of the invention of printing by Johann Gutenberg.

Hark! the herald angels sing
Glory to the new-born King,
Peace on earth, and mercy mild,
God and sinners reconciled.
Joyful, all ye nations rise,
Join the triumph of the skies;
With the angelic host proclaim,
'Christ is born in Bethlehem.'

Hark! the herald angels sing
Glory to the new-born King.

Christ, by highest heaven adored,
Christ, the everlasting Lord,
Late in time behold Him come,
Offspring of a virgin's womb.
Veiled in flesh the Godhead see!
Hail, the incarnate deity!
Pleased as man with man to dwell,
Jesus, our Emmanuel.

Hail, the heaven-born Prince of peace!
Hail, the sun of righteousness!
Light and life to all He brings,
Risen with healing in His wings,
Mild He lays His glory by,
Born that man no more may die,
Born to raise the sons of earth,
Born to give them second birth.

Charles Wesley (1707–88)

He's got the whole world in His hand

This is one of the handful of songs regularly sung at modern Christingle services. The tune, arranged by James Whitburn (b.1963), is traditional and the repetitive structure owes much to the spirituals of the American South.

He's got the whole world in His hand,
He's got the whole wide world in His hand,
He's got the whole world in His hand,
He's got the whole world in His hand.

He's got you and me, brother, in His hand,
He's got you and me, brother, in His hand,
He's got you and me, brother, in His hand,
He's got the whole world in His hand.

He's got you and me, sister, in His hand,
He's got you and me, sister, in His hand,
He's got you and me, sister, in His hand,
He's got the whole world in His hand.

He's got the whole world in His hand,
He's got the whole wide world in His hand,
He's got the whole world in His hand,
He's got the whole world in His hand.

Anonymous

The holly and the ivy

*This carol is a traditional English song and was included in the folk
songs collected by musicologist Cecil Sharp in 1911. Sharp heard it from a
Mrs Mary Clayton of Chipping Camden in Gloucestershire, though it is
thought to be centuries older. Holly and ivy were symbols of victory in the
Celtic culture and have retained their ancient links with Christmas
festivities ever since.*

The holly and the ivy,
When they are both full grown,
Of all the trees that are in the wood,
The holly bears the crown.
*The rising of the sun
And the running of the deer,
The playing of the merry organ,
Sweet singing in the choir.*

The holly bears a blossom
As white as the lily flower,
And Mary bore sweet Jesus Christ
To be our sweet Saviour.

The holly bears a berry
As red as any blood,
And Mary bore sweet Jesus Christ
To do poor sinners good.

The holly bears a prickle
As sharp as any thorn,
And Mary bore sweet Jesus Christ
On Christmas Day in the morn.

The holly bears a bark
As bitter as any gall,
And Mary bore sweet Jesus Christ
For to redeem us all.

The holly and the ivy,
When they are both full grown,
Of all the trees that are in the wood,
The holly bears the crown.

Anonymous

Hymn on the morning of Christ's nativity

These verses come from a much longer poem by John Milton on the theme of Christ's birth. In response to the momentous event, the world hides its flaws under snow and war is at least temporarily replaced by peace.

It was the Winter wilde,
While the Heav'n-born-childe,
All meanly wrapt in the rude manger lies;
Nature in aw to him
Had dofft her gawdy trim,
With her great Master so to sympathize:
It was no season then for her
To wanton with the Sun her lusty Paramour.

Only with speeches fair
She woos the gentle Air
To hide her guilty front with innocent Snow,
And on her naked shame,
Pollute with sinfull blame,
The Saintly Vail of Maiden white to throw,
Confounded, that her Makers eyes
Should look so neer upon her foul deformities.

But he her fears to cease,
Sent down the meek-eyd Peace,
She crown'd with Olive green, came softly sliding
Down through the turning sphear
His ready Harbinger,
With Turtle wing the amorous clouds dividing,
And waving wide her myrtle wand,
She strikes a universall Peace through Sea and Land.

No Warr, or Battails sound
Was heard the World around,
The idle spear and shield were high up hung;
The hooked Chariot stood
Unstain'd with hostile blood,
The Trumpet spake not to the armed throng,
And Kings sate still with awfull eye,
As if they surely knew their Sovran Lord was by.

But peacefull was the night
Wherin the Prince of light
His raign of peace upon the earth began:
The Windes with wonder whist,
Smoothly the waters kist,
Whispering new joyes to the milde Ocean,
Who now hath quite forgot to rave,
While Birds of Calm sit brooding on the charmed wave . . .

. . . But see the Virgin blest,
Hath laid her Babe to rest.
Time is our tedious Song should here have ending,
Heav'ns youngest teemed Star
Hath fixt her polisht Car,
Her sleeping Lord with Handmaid Lamp attending:
And all about the Courtly Stable,
Bright-harnest Angels sit in order serviceable.

   John Milton (1608–74)

I am the way

These words, from John 14:1–13, are often quoted as an illustration of God's assurance that the faithful will be rewarded with a place in heaven. They point to the fact that Jesus Christ is the only way to the Father. The reading confirms the intimate relationship between Christ and God the Father.

'Do not let your hearts be troubled. Believe in God, believe also in me. In my Father's house there are many dwelling-places. If it were not so, would I have told you that I go to prepare a place for you? And if I go and prepare a place for you, I will come again and will take you to myself, so that where I am, there you may be also. And you know the way to the place where I am going.' Thomas said to him, 'Lord, we do not know where you are going. How can we know the way?' Jesus said to him, 'I am the way, and the truth, and the life. No one comes to the Father except through me. If you know me, you will know my Father also. From now on you do know him and have seen him.'

Philip said to him, 'Lord, show us the Father, and we will be satisfied.' Jesus said to him, 'Have I been with you all this time, Philip, and you still do not know me? Whoever has seen me has seen the Father. How can you say, "Show us the Father"? Do you not believe that I am in the Father and the Father is in me? The words that I say to you I do not speak on my own; but the Father who dwells in me does his works. Believe me that I am in the Father and the Father is in me; but if you do not, then believe me because of the works themselves. Very truly, I tell you, the one who believes in me will also do the works that I do and, in fact, will do greater works than these, because I am going to the Father. I will do whatever you ask in my name, so that the Father may be glorified in the Son.'

I saw three ships come sailing in

This carol is known in a number of forms, all of which take as their inspiration the legendary travels of the relics of the magi. The earliest published version of these lines appeared in 1666. Another popular version gives the carol the title 'Sunny bank'.

I saw three ships come sailing in
On Christmas Day, on Christmas Day,
I saw three ships come sailing in
On Christmas Day in the morning.

And what was in those ships all three?
On Christmas Day, on Christmas Day,
And what was in those ships all three?
On Christmas Day in the morning.

Our Saviour Christ and his lady,
On Christmas Day, on Christmas Day,
Our Saviour Christ and his lady,
On Christmas Day in the morning.

Pray, whither sailed those ships all three?
On Christmas Day, on Christmas Day,
Pray, whither sailed those ships all three?
On Christmas Day in the morning.

O they sailed into Bethlehem
On Christmas Day, on Christmas Day,
O they sailed into Bethlehem
On Christmas Day in the morning.

And all the bells on earth shall ring
On Christmas Day, on Christmas Day,
And all the bells on earth shall ring
On Christmas Day in the morning.

And all the angels in heaven shall sing
On Christmas Day, on Christmas Day,
And all the angels in heaven shall sing
On Christmas Day in the morning.

And all the souls on earth shall sing
On Christmas Day, on Christmas Day,
And all the souls on earth shall sing
On Christmas Day in the morning.

Then let us all rejoice amain
On Christmas Day, on Christmas Day,
Then let us all rejoice amain
On Christmas Day in the morning.

Anonymous

I sing of a maiden

This anonymous poem in praise of the Virgin Mary dates from the fifteenth century.

I sing of a maiden
That is makeles;
King of all kings
To her son she ches.

He came al so still
There his mother was,
As dew in April
That falleth on the grass.

He came al so still
To his mother's bour,
As dew in April
That falleth on the flour.

He came al so still
There his mother lay,
As dew in April
That falleth on the spray.

Mother and maiden
Was never none but she;
Well may such a lady
Goddes mother be.

    Anonymous

In the beginning was the Word

This passage, from John 1:1–14, is among the most famous of Bible readings. The descriptions of 'a light shining in the darkness' and 'the Word became flesh and lived among us' remain two of the most memorable in Christian theology. The appropriate response is to receive Christ – to believe in his name – and so become children of God.

In the beginning was the Word, and the Word was with God, and the Word was God. He was in the beginning with God. All things came into being through him, and without him not one thing came into being. What has come into being in him was life, and the life was the light of all people. The light shines in the darkness, and the darkness did not overcome it.

There was a man sent from God, whose name was John. He came as a witness to testify to the light, so that all might believe through him. He himself was not the light, but he came to testify to the light. The true light, which enlightens everyone, was coming into the world.

He was in the world, and the world came into being through him; yet the world did not know him. He came to what was his own, and his own people did not accept him. But to all who received him, who believed in his name, he gave power to become children of God, who were born, not of blood or of the will of the flesh or of the will of man, but of God.

And the Word became flesh and lived among us, and we have seen his glory, the glory as of a father's only son, full of grace and truth.

In the bleak mid-winter

Christina Rossetti did not write these verses specifically to be sung, and some of the credit for the enduring popularity of this carol should go to the composer Gustav Holst (1874–1934), who contributed the tune to which Rossetti's metrically uneven lines are usually sung today.

In the bleak mid-winter
Frosty wind made moan,
Earth stood hard as iron,
Water like a stone:
Snow had fallen, snow on snow,
Snow on snow,
In the bleak mid-winter,
Long ago.

Our God, heaven cannot hold him
Nor earth sustain:
Heaven and earth shall flee away
When he comes to reign:
In the bleak mid-winter
A stable place sufficed
The Lord God almighty
Jesus Christ.

Enough for him, whom cherubim
Worship night and day,
A breastful of milk
And a mangerful of hay:
Enough for him, whom angels
Fall down before,
The ox and ass and camel
Which adore.

What can I give him,
Poor as I am?
If I were a shepherd
I would bring a lamb;
If I were a wise man
I would do my part;
Yet what I can I give him
Give my heart, give my heart.

Christina Rossetti (1830–94)

Infant holy, infant lowly

This is a traditional Polish carol that dates possibly from the thirteenth century. It has since become widely popular in translation in the English-speaking world.

Infant holy, Infant lowly,
For his bed a cattle-stall;
Oxen lowing, little knowing
Christ the Babe is Lord of all.
Swiftly winging angels singing,
Nowells ringing, tidings bringing:
Christ the Babe is Lord of all.

Flocks were sleeping, shepherds keeping
Vigil till the morning new;
Saw the glory, heard the story,
Tidings of a gospel true.
Thus rejoicing, free from sorrow,
Praises voicing, greet the morrow:
Christ the Babe was born for you.

Anonymous, translated by Edith M. G. Reed (1885–1933)

Permission has been sought.

It came upon a midnight clear

The words of this lastingly popular carol were written by a Unitarian clergyman called Edmund H. Sears. His words are today usually sung to a setting by the celebrated English composer Arthur Sullivan (1842–1900), who is said to have devised the tune on the basis of a short melody volunteered by a friend.

It came upon a midnight clear,
That glorious song of old,
From angels, bending near the earth
To touch their harps of gold:
'Peace on the earth, goodwill to men
From heaven's all-gracious King!'
The world in solemn stillness lay
To hear the angels sing.

Still through the cloven skies they come,
With peaceful wings unfurled,
And still their heavenly music floats
O'er all the weary world:
Above its sad and lowly plains
They bend on hovering wing,
And ever o'er its Babel sounds
The blessed angels sing.

Yet with the woes of sin and strife
The world has suffered long:
Beneath the angels' strain have rolled
Two thousand years of wrong,
And man, at war with man, hears not
The love-song which they bring:
O hush the noise, ye men of strife,
And hear the angels sing!

And ye, beneath life's crushing load,
Whose forms are bending low,
Who toil along the climbing way
With painful steps and slow,
Look now! for glad and golden hours
Come swiftly on the wing;
O rest beside the weary road,
And hear the angels sing!

For lo! the days are hastening on,
By prophet-bards foretold,
When, with the ever-circling years,
Comes round the Age of Gold,
When peace shall over all the earth
Its ancient splendours fling,
And the whole world give back the song
Which now the angels sing.

Edmund H. Sears (1810–76)

It's rounded like an orange

*Sung to the same tune as 'The holly and the ivy', these verses have become
a feature of the modern Christingle service, hence the alternative title
'The Christingle carol'. Children and other attendants at Christingle services
hold a lighted candle mounted in an orange, representing the world.*

It's rounded like an orange,
This earth on which we stand;
And we praise the God who holds it
In the hollow of his hand.

*So Father, we would thank you
For all that you have done,
And for all that you have given us
Through the coming of your Son.*

A candle, burning brightly,
Can cheer the darkest night
And these candles tell how Jesus
Came to bring a dark world light.

The ribbon round the orange
Reminds us of the cost;
How the Shepherd, strong and gentle,
Gave His life to save the lost.

Four seasons with their harvest
Supply the food we need,
And the Spirit gives a harvest
That can make us rich indeed.

We come with our Christingles
To tell of Jesus' birth
And we praise the God who blessed us
By his coming to this earth.

Basil Bridge (b.1927)

*Words by Basil Bridge (1927–) © 1990 Oxford University Press from
'New Songs of Praise 5'. Reproduced by permission.*

Jesus Christ is Lord

These words, from Philippians 2:5–11, commend Christ as the model of ideal Christian virtue. He is the supreme example of humility whom we should imitate. Christ set aside his glory to become a servant. He submitted to the humiliation of becoming human and, in obedience to the Father, died for us. God's purpose is that everyone should worship and serve Christ as Lord.

Let the same mind be in you that was in Christ Jesus, who, though he was in the form of God, did not regard equality with God as something to be exploited, but emptied himself, taking the form of a slave, being born in human likeness. And being found in human form, he humbled himself and became obedient to the point of death – even death on a cross.

Therefore God also highly exalted him and gave him the name that is above every name, so that at the name of Jesus every knee should bend, in heaven and on earth and under the earth, and every tongue should confess that Jesus Christ is Lord, to the glory of God the Father.

Jingle bells

According to legend, this ubiquitous Christmas song (originally entitled 'One-horse open sleigh') was written in 1857 by the organist James Pierpont to be sung at a Thanksgiving service in Boston. Such was the enthusiasm with which it was received that it was repeated there that Christmas, setting it on its way to becoming a Christmas standard. Another tradition has it that Pierpont (sometimes described as a rebellious character with a bad reputation) actually wrote the song in a Massachusetts tavern or, alternatively, in Savannah, Georgia, while pining for the New England of his childhood. Despite the absence of any religious overtones, it is now one of the most familiar of all Christmas songs, heard both inside and outside church (though it is rarely sung in full).

Dashing through the snow
In a one-horse open sleigh
O'er the fields we go
Laughing all the way.
Bells on bob-tail ring
Making spirits bright
What fun it is to ride and sing
A sleighing song tonight.

Jingle bells, jingle bells
Jingle all the way,
Oh what fun it is to ride
In a one-horse open sleigh,
Oh jingle bells, jingle bells
Jingle all the way,
Oh what fun it is to ride
In a one-horse open sleigh.

A day or two ago
I thought I'd take a ride
And soon Miss Fanny Bright
Was seated by my side;
The horse was lean and lank
Misfortune seemed his lot,
We ran into a drifted bank
And there we got upset.

A day or two ago
The story I must tell
I went out on the snow
And on my back I fell;
A gent was riding by
In a one-horse open sleigh
He laughed at me as
I there sprawling laid
But quickly drove away.

Now the ground is white,
Go it while you're young,
Take the girls along
And sing this sleighing song.
Just bet a bob-tailed bay,
Two-forty as his speed,
Hitch him to an open sleigh
And crack! You'll take the lead.

James Lord Pierpont (1822–93)

Joly Wat

This is an English ballad dating from the medieval period. Joly Wat is the name given here to the good-natured shepherd who responds to the birth of Christ by offering him his most prized possession.

Can I not sing but 'Hoy',
Whan the joly Shepard made so much joy?

The Shepard upon a hill he sat;
He had on him his tabard and his hat,
His tarbox, his pipe, and his flagat;
His name was called Joly Joly Wat,
For he was a gud herdes boy.
Ut hoy!
For in his pipe he made so much joy.

The Shepard upon a hill was laid;
His dog unto his girdell was taid;
He had not slept but a litill braid;
But "Gloria in excelsis" was to him said.
Ut hoy!
For in his pipe he made so much joy.

The Shepard on a hill he stode;
Round about him his shepe they yode;
He put his hond under his hode,
He saw a star as rede as blode.
Ut hoy!
For in his pipe he made so much joy.

The Shepard said anon right,
'I will go see yon ferly sight,
Whereas the angel singeth on hight,
And the star that shineth so bright.'
Ut hoy!
For in his pipe he made so much joy.

'Now farewell, Mall, and also Will!
For my love go ye all still

Unto I cum again you till,
And evermore, Will, ring well thy bell.'
Ut hoy!
For in his pipe he made so much joy.

'Now must I go there Crist was born;
Farewell! I cum again to-morn.
Dog, kepe well my shepe fro the corn,
And warn well "Warroke" when I blow my horn!'
Ut hoy!
For in his pipe he made so much joy.

Whan Wat to Bedlem cumen was
He swet, he had gone faster than a pace;
He found Jesu in a simpell place,
Between an ox but and an asse.
Ut hoy!
For in his pipe he made so much joy.

'Jesu, I offer to thee here my pipe,
My skirt, my tarbox, and my scrip;
Home to my felowes now will I skip,
And also look unto my shepe.'
Ut hoy!
For in his pipe he made so much joy.

'Now faresell, mine owne herdsman Wat!' –
'Yea, for God, lady, even so I hat;
Lull well Jesu in thy lap,
And farewell, Joseph, with thy round cap!'
Ut hoy!
For in his pipe he made so much joy.

'Now may I well both hope and sing,
For I have bene at Cristes bering;
Home to my felowes now will I fling.
Crist of heven to his bliss us bring!'
Ut hoy!
For in his pipe he made so much joy.

Anonymous

Joseph and Mary

These words from Matthew 1:18–25 describe how Joseph found out from an angelic visitation that Mary was to give birth to the infant Christ. He would be called Jesus, which means 'the Lord saves'. This particular passage is often recited in the course of Christmas services.

Now the birth of Jesus the Messiah took place in this way. When his mother Mary had been engaged to Joseph, but before they lived together, she was found to be with child from the Holy Spirit. Her husband Joseph, being a righteous man and unwilling to expose her to public disgrace, planned to dismiss her quietly. But just when he had resolved to do this, an angel of the Lord appeared to him in a dream and said, 'Joseph, son of David, do not be afraid to take Mary as your wife, for the child conceived in her is from the Holy Spirit. She will bear a son, and you are to name him Jesus, for he will save his people from their sins.' All this took place to fulfil what had been spoken by the Lord through the prophet: 'Look, the virgin shall conceive and bear a son, and they shall name him Emmanuel', which means, 'God is with us.' When Joseph awoke from sleep, he did as the angel of the Lord commanded him; he took her as his wife, but had no marital relations with her until she had borne a son; and he named him Jesus.

Journey of the magi

In this celebrated poem, T. S. Eliot depicts the three magi travelling to worship the infant Christ. Their winter journey is brought to life through a series of memorable details, but the essence of the poem is the speculation of the narrator, one of the magi, upon the nature of the great event they have witnessed.

'A cold coming we had of it,
Just the worst time of the year
For a journey, and such a long journey:
'The ways deep and the weather sharp,
The very dead of winter.'
And the camels galled, sore-footed, refractory,
Lying down in the melting snow.
There were times we regretted
The summer palaces on slopes, the terraces,
And the silken girls bringing sherbet.
Then the camel men cursing and grumbling
And running away, and wanting their liquor and women,
And the night-fires going out, and the lack of shelters,
And the cities hostile and the towns unfriendly
And the villages dirty and charging high prices:
A hard time we had of it.
At the end we preferred to travel all night,
Sleeping in snatches,
With the voices singing in our ears, saying
That this was all folly.

Then at dawn we came down to a temperate valley,
Wet, below the snow line, smelling of vegetation,
With a running stream and a water-mill beating the darkness,
And three trees on the low sky.
And an old white horse galloped away in the meadow.
Then we came to a tavern with vine-leaves over the lintel,
Six hands at an open door dicing for pieces of silver,
And feet kicking the empty wine-skins.
But there was no information, and so we continued
And arrived at evening, not a moment too soon
Finding the place; it was (you may say) satisfactory.

All this was a long time ago, I remember,
And I would do it again, but set down
This set down
This: were we led all that way for
Birth or Death? There was a Birth, certainly,
We had evidence and no doubt. I had seen birth and death,
But had thought they were different; this Birth was
Hard and bitter agony for us, like Death, our death.
We returned to our places, these Kingdoms,
But no longer at ease here, in the old dispensation,
With an alien people clutching their gods.
I should be glad of another death.

T. S. Eliot (1888–1965)

Permission has been sought.

Joy to the world

This Christmas hymn by Isaac Watts was written in response to a challenge by his father. The fifteen-year-old Isaac had complained to his father, a deacon at a Southampton church, about the lack of vigour in the congregation's singing and was consequently set the task of writing something that would rouse their enthusiasm. The resulting hymn has become a firm Christmas favourite, despite the fact that it does not refer directly to Christ's birth. It is based on Psalm 98, which summons the world to celebrate the coming of the Lord.

Joy to the world, the Lord has come!
Let earth receive her King;
Let every heart prepare Him room,
And heaven and nature sing.

Joy to the earth, the Saviour reigns!
Your sweetest songs employ;
While fields and floods, rocks, hills and plains
Repeat the sounding joy.

No more let sins and sorrows grow,
Nor thorus infest the ground;
He comes to make His blessings flow
Far as the curse is found.

He rules the world with truth and grace,
And makes the nations prove
The glories of His righteousness,
The wonders of His love.

Isaac Watts (1647–1748)

King John's Christmas

In this poem, it is clear that the anxieties and excitements of Christmas are
open to all, even to the most undeserving.

King John was not a good man –
He had his little ways.
And sometimes no one spoke to him
For days and days and days.
And men who came across him,
When walking in the town,
Gave him a supercilious stare,
Or passed with noses in the air –
And bad King John stood dumbly there,
Blushing beneath his crown.

King John was not a good man,
And no good friends had he.
He stayed in every afternoon . . .
But no one came to tea.
And, round about December,
The cards upon his shelf
Which wished him lots of Christmas cheer,
And fortune in the coming year,
Were never from his near and dear,
But only from himself.

King John was not a good man,
Yet had his hopes and fears.
They'd given him no present now
For years and years and years.
But every year at Christmas,
While minstrels stood about,
Collecting tribute from the young
For all the songs they might have sung,
He stole away upstairs and hung
A hopeful stocking out.

King John was not a good man,
He lived his life aloof;
Alone he thought a message out
While climbing up the roof.
He wrote it down and propped it
Against the chimney stack:
'TO ALL AND SUNDRY – NEAR AND FAR –
F. CHRISTMAS IN PARTICULAR.'
And signed it not 'Johannes R.'
But very humbly, 'JACK.'

'I want some crackers,
And I want some candy;
I think a box of chocolates
Would come in handy;
I don't mind oranges,
I do like nuts!
And I SHOULD like a pocket-knife
That really cuts.
And, oh! Father Christmas, if you love me at all,
Bring me a big, red india-rubber ball!'

King John was not a good man –
He wrote this message out,
And gat him to his room again,
Descending by the spout.
And all that night he lay there,
A prey to hopes and fears.
'I think that's him a-coming now,'
(Anxiety bedewed his brow.)
'He'll bring one present, anyhow –
The first I've had for years.'

'Forget about the crackers,
And forget about the candy;
I'm sure a box of chocolates
Would never come in handy;
I don't like oranges,
I don't want nuts,
And I HAVE got a pocket-knife
That almost cuts.
But, oh! Father Christmas, if you love me at all,
Bring me a big, red india-rubber ball!'

King John was not a good man –
Next morning when the sun
Rose up to tell a waiting world
That Christmas had begun,
And people seized their stockings,
And opened them with glee,
And crackers, toys and games appeared,
And lips with sticky sweets were smeared,
King John said grimly: 'As I feared,
Nothing again for me!'

'I did want crackers,
And I did want candy;
I know a box of chocolates
Would come in handy;
I do love oranges,
I did want nuts.
I haven't got a pocket-knife –
Not one that cuts.
And, oh! if Father Christmas had loved me at all,
He would have brought a big, red india-rubber ball!'

King John stood by the window,
And frowned to see below
The happy bands of boys and girls
All playing in the snow.
A while he stood there watching,
And envying them all . . .
When through the window big and red
There hurtled by his royal head,
And bounced and fell upon the bed,
An india-rubber ball!"

AND OH, FATHER CHRISTMAS,
MY BLESSINGS ON YOU FALL
FOR BRINGING HIM
A BIG, RED,
INDIA-RUBBER
BALL!

A. A. Milne (1882–1956)

From Now We Are Six © A A Milne. Published by Egmont UK Limited, London and used with permission. Published in the US and Canada by Penguin. Used with permission.

Lady selecting her Christmas cards

This poem celebrates one of the rites of the modern Christmas, the task of writing and sending Christmas cards. McGinley here makes a point of reminding the reader what they are really about.

Fastidiously, with gloved and careful fingers,
Through the marked samples she pursues her search.
Which shall it be: the snowscape's wintry languors
Complete with church,

An urban skyline, children sweetly pretty
Sledding downhill, the chaste ubiquitous wreath,
Schooner or candle or simple Scottie
With verse underneath?

Perhaps it might be better to emblazon
With words alone the stiff, punctilious square.
(Oh, not Victorian certainly. This season
One meets it everywhere.)

She has a duty proper to the weather –
A Birth she must announce, a rumour to spread,
Wherefore the very spheres once sang together
And a star shone overhead.

Here are the tidings which the shepherds panted
One to another, kneeling by their flocks.
And they will bear her name (engraved, not printed),
Twelve-fifty for the box.

Phyllis McGinley (1905–78)

A light to the nations

This passage, from Isaiah 49:1–18, is one of the 'servant songs' in Isaiah, in which the servant is the Messiah. Christians see these words as ultimately fulfilled in Jesus, the light of the world and the Redeemer. God loves his people and remains committed to their welfare.

Listen to me, O coastlands, pay attention, you peoples from far away! The LORD called me before I was born, while I was in my mother's womb he named me. He made my mouth like a sharp sword, in the shadow of his hand he hid me; he made me a polished arrow, in his quiver he hid me away. And he said to me, 'You are my servant, Israel, in whom I will be glorified.' But I said, 'I have laboured in vain, I have spent my strength for nothing and vanity; yet surely my cause is with the Lord, and my reward with my God.'

And now the LORD says, who formed me in the womb to be his servant, to bring Jacob back to him, and that Israel might be gathered to him, for I am honoured in the sight of the LORD, and my God has become my strength – he says, 'It is too light a thing that you should be my servant to raise up the tribes of Jacob and to restore the survivors of Israel; I will give you as a light to the nations, that my salvation may reach to the end of the earth.'

Thus says the LORD, the Redeemer of Israel and his Holy One, to one deeply despised, abhorred by the nations, the slave of rulers, 'Kings shall see and stand up, princes, and they shall prostrate themselves, because of the LORD, who is faithful, the Holy One of Israel, who has chosen you.'

Thus says the LORD: In a time of favour I have answered you, on a day of salvation I have helped you; I have kept you and given you as a covenant to the people, to establish the land, to apportion the desolate heritages; saying to the prisoners, 'Come out', to those who are in darkness, 'Show yourselves.' They shall feed along the ways, on all the bare heights shall be their pasture; they shall not hunger or thirst, neither scorching wind nor sun shall strike them down, for he who has pity on them will lead them, and by springs of water will guide them. And I will turn all my mountains into a road, and my highways shall be raised up. Lo, these shall come from far away, and lo, these from the north and from the west, and these from the land of Syene.

Sing for joy, O heavens, and exult, O earth; break forth, O mountains, into singing! For the LORD has comforted his people, and will have compassion on his suffering ones.

But Zion said, 'The LORD has forsaken me, my LORD has forgotten me.' Can a woman forget her nursing-child, or show no compassion for the child of her womb? Even these may forget, yet I will not forget you. See, I have inscribed you on the palms of my hands; your walls are continually before me. Your builders outdo your destroyers, and those who laid you waste go away from you. Lift up your eyes all around and see; they all gather, they come to you. As I live, says the LORD, you shall put all of them on like an ornament, and like a bride you shall bind them on.

A little child

This simple poem by an unidentified author expresses the Christmas message in an endearingly uncomplicated manner.

A little child,
A shining star,
A stable rude,
The door ajar,
Yet in this place,
So crude, forlorn,
The Hope of all
The world was born.

    Anonymous

little tree

The Christmas tree, popularised in Britain in the nineteenth century by Queen Victoria's consort Prince Albert, symbolises the magic of Christmas. In this poem the tree is imagined as a living thing with feelings and fears of its own.

little tree
little silent Christmas tree
you are so little
you are more like a flower

who found you in the green forest
and were you very sorry to come away?
see   i will comfort you
because you smell so sweetly

i will kiss your cool bark
and hug you safe and tight
just as your mother would,
only don't be afraid

look   the spangles
that sleep all the year in a dark box
dreaming of being taken out and allowed to shine,
the balls the chains red and gold the fluffy threads,

put up your little arms
and i'll give them all to you to hold
every finger shall have its ring
and there won't be a single place dark or unhappy

then when you're quite dressed
you'll stand in the window for everyone to see
and how they'll stare!
oh but you'll be very proud

and my little sister and i will take hands
and looking up at our beautiful tree
we'll dance and sing
'Noel Noel'

E. E. Cummings (1894–1962)

Lo! He comes with clouds descending

This Advent hymn was adapted by Charles Wesley in 1758 from an existing hymn written by his contemporary John Cennick. It is usually sung to the tune 'Helmsley' by Thomas Olivers (1725–99). Tradition has it that Olivers wrote his famous tune after hearing something like it being whistled in the street (although it seems more likely that he based it on a concert-room song entitled 'Guardian angels, now protect me'). The hymn subsequently became a particular favourite of Queen Victoria.

Lo! He comes with clouds descending,
Once for favoured sinners slain;
Thousand, thousand saints, attending,
Swell the triumph of His train.
Hallelujah! hallelujah! hallelujah!
God appear on earth to reign.

Every eye shall now behold Him
Robed in dreadful majesty;
Those who set at nought and sold Him,
Pierced, and nailed Him to the tree,
Deeply wailing, deeply wailing,
Shall the true Messiah see.

Every island, sea, and mountain,
Heaven, and earth, shall flee away;
All who hate Him must, confounded,
Hear the trump proclaim the Day:
Come to judgement! Come to judgement!
Come to judgement! Come away!

Now Redemption, long expected,
See in solemn pomp appear!
All His saints, by man rejected,
Now shall meet Him in the air!
Hallelujah! hallelujah!
See the Day of God appear!

Answer Thine own Bride and Spirit,
Hasten, Lord, the general doom!
The new heaven and earth to inherit,
Take Thy pining exiles home!
All creation, all creation,
Travails, groans, and bids Thee come!

The dear tokens of His Passion
Still His dazzling body bears,
Cause of endless exultation
To His ransomed worshippers:
With what rapture, with what rapture,
Gaze we on those glorious scars!

Yea, amen! let all adore Thee,
High on Thy eternal throne!
Saviour, take the power and glory:
Claim the kingdom for Thine own!
O come quickly! O come quickly!
Hallelujah! come, Lord, come!

Charles Wesley (1707–88) and
John Cennick (1718–55)

Love came down at Christmas

This popular carol was penned by the celebrated poet Christina Rossetti sometime before 1886 and remains one of her best-loved works.

Love came down at Christmas,
Love all lovely, love divine;
Love was born at Christmas,
Star and angels gave the sign.

Worship we the Godhead,
Love incarnate, love divine;
Worship we our Jesus:
But wherewith for sacred sign?

Love shall be our token,
Love by yours and love be mine,
Love to God and all men,
Love for plea and gift and sign.

Christina Rossetti (1830–94)

The Magnificat

This passage, from Luke 1:39–56, recalls the delight shared by the expectant mothers Mary and Elizabeth at the realisation that their children have been sent by God. The word 'Magnificat' comes from the Latin: 'My soul magnifies the Lord'. It is often read in services in the days leading up to Christmas.

In those days Mary set out and went with haste to a Judean town in the hill country, where she entered the house of Zechariah and greeted Elizabeth. When Elizabeth heard Mary's greeting, the child leapt in her womb. And Elizabeth was filled with the Holy Spirit and exclaimed with a loud cry, 'Blessed are you among women, and blessed is the fruit of your womb. And why has this happened to me, that the mother of my Lord comes to me? For as soon as I heard the sound of your greeting, the child in my womb leapt for joy. And blessed is she who believed that there would be a fulfilment of what was spoken to her by the Lord.'

And Mary said, 'My soul magnifies the Lord, and my spirit rejoices in God my Saviour, for he has looked with favour on the lowliness of his servant. Surely, from now on all generations will call me blessed; for the Mighty One has done great things for me, and holy is his name. His mercy is for those who fear him from generation to generation. He has shown strength with his arm; he has scattered the proud in the thoughts of their hearts. He has brought down the powerful from their thrones, and lifted up the lowly; he has filled the hungry with good things, and sent the rich away empty. He has helped his servant Israel, in remembrance of his mercy, according to the promise he made to our ancestors, to Abraham and to his descendants for ever.'

And Mary remained with her for about three months and then returned to her home.

Mary had a baby

*This Christmas spiritual was collected on the island of St Helena by
N.G. J. Ballanta-Taylor in 1925. It has since become one of the more popular
post-Victorian Christmas songs. The question-and-answer structure is typical
of the spiritual form.*

Mary had a baby, Aye, Lord,
Mary had a baby, Aye, my Lord,
Mary had a baby, Aye, Lord,
The people keep a-comin' and the train done gone.

Where did she lay him? Aye, Lord,
Where did she lay him? Aye, my Lord,
Where did she lay him? Aye, Lord,
The people keep a-comin' and the train done gone.

Laid him in a manger, Aye, Lord,
Laid him in a manger, Aye, my Lord,
Laid him in a manger, Aye, Lord,
The people keep a-comin' and the train done gone.

What did she name him? Aye, Lord,
What did she name him? Aye, my Lord,
What did she name him? Aye, Lord,
The people keep a-comin' and the train done gone.

Name him King Jesus, Aye, Lord,
Name him King Jesus, Aye, my Lord,
Name him King Jesus, Aye, Lord,
The people keep a-comin' and the train done gone.

Who heard the singin'? Aye, Lord,
Who heard the singin'? Aye, my Lord,
Who heard the singin'? Aye, Lord,
The people keep a-comin' and the train done gone.

Shepherds heard the singin', Aye, Lord,
Shepherds heard the singin', Aye, my Lord,
Shepherds heard the singin', Aye, Lord,
The people keep a-comin' and the train done gone.

Star keep a-shining, Aye, Lord,
Star keep a-shining, Aye, my Lord,
Star keep a-shining, Aye, Lord,
The people keep a-comin' and the train done gone.

Moving in the elements, Aye, Lord,
Moving in the elements, Aye, my Lord,
Moving in the elements, Aye, Lord,
The people keep a-comin' and the train done gone.

Jesus went to Egypt, Aye, Lord,
Jesus went to Egypt, Aye, my Lord,
Jesus went to Egypt, Aye, Lord,
The people keep a-comin' and the train done gone.

Travelled on a donkey, Aye, Lord,
Travelled on a donkey, Aye, my Lord,
Travelled on a donkey, Aye, Lord,
The people keep a-comin' and the train done gone.

Angels went around him, Aye, Lord,
Angels went around him, Aye, my Lord,
Angels went around him, Aye, Lord,
The people keep a-comin' and the train done gone.

Anonymous

The messenger of God

This passage, from Malachi 3:1–4, conveys God's promise to send his Son to the world. 'My messenger' refers to John the Baptist, sent to prepare the way for the Lord. When the Lord comes, he will purify his people. This reading is sometimes quoted in services as an introduction to the Christmas story.

See, I am sending my messenger to prepare the way before me, and the LORD whom you seek will suddenly come to his temple. The messenger of the covenant in whom you delight – indeed, he is coming, says the LORD of hosts. But who can endure the day of his coming, and who can stand when he appears?

For he is like a refiner's fire and like fullers' soap; he will sit as a refiner and purifier of silver, and he will purify the descendants of Levi and refine them like gold and silver, until they present offerings to the LORD in righteousness. Then the offering of Judah and Jerusalem will be pleasing to the LORD as in the days of old and as in former years.

Minstrel's song

The birth of Christ is described in this poem through the agency of a minstrel who has been sleeping in the stable where Christ is born. His sense of wonder encapsulates the feelings of many churchgoers at this time of year.

I've just had an astounding dream as I lay in the straw.
I dreamed a star fell on to the straw beside me
And lay blazing. Then when I looked up
I saw a bull come flying through a sky of fire
And on its shoulders a huge silver woman
Holding the moon. And afterwards there came
A donkey flying through that same burning heaven
And on its shoulders a colossal man
Holding the sun. Suddenly I awoke
And saw a bull and a donkey kneeling in the straw,
And the great moving shadows of a man and a woman –
I say they were a man and a woman but
I dare not say what I think they were. I did not dare to look.
I ran out here into the freezing world
Because I dared not look. Inside that shed.
A star is coming this way along the road.
If I were not standing upright, this would be a dream.
A star the shape of a sword of fire, point-downward,
Is floating along the road. And now it rises.
It is shaking fire on to the roofs and gardens.
And now it rises above the animal shed
Where I slept till the dream woke me. And now
The star is standing over the animal shed.

Ted Hughes (1930–98)

Permission has been sought.

Mistletoe

Mistletoe has long played a unique role in Christmas festivities as a traditional feature of the decorations. People have kissed beneath the mistletoe at Christmas since Saxon times at least, believing the plant to promote sexual potency. Considered magical by ancient druids, mistletoe is not included among the plants used to decorate churches at Christmas because of these pagan associations.

Sitting under the mistletoe
(Pale green, fairy mistletoe)
One last candle burning low,
All the sleepy dancers gone,
Just one candle burning on,
Shadows lurking everywhere:
Someone came, and kissed me there.

Tired I was; my head would go
Nodding under the mistletoe
(Pale green, fairy mistletoe)
No footstep came, no voice, but only,
Just as I sat there, sleepy, lonely,
Stooped in the still and shadowy air,
Lips unseen – and kissed me there.

Walter de la Mare (1873–1956)

The mystery of our religion

This biblical passage comes from 1 Timothy 3:14–16. Its simple but eloquent summary of Christ's impact upon the world sums up the importance of what we celebrate with the festivities of Christmas. The words of verse 16 ('He was revealed . . .') may well come from an early Christian hymn.

I hope to come to you soon, but I am writing these instructions to you so that, if I am delayed, you may know how one ought to behave in the household of God, which is the church of the living God, the pillar and bulwark of the truth. Without any doubt, the mystery of our religion is great:

He was revealed in flesh, vindicated in spirit, seen by angels, proclaimed among Gentiles, believed in throughout the world, taken up in glory.

The night before Christmas

Clement C. Moore, an American classical scholar, composed this greatly loved Christmas poem to amuse his children. The story goes that he was much dismayed when the poem (originally entitled 'A Visit from Saint Nicholas') appeared in print, having been published by a friend of the family who had been captivated by it. Fearing his reputation as a serious scholar would be damaged by it, Moore refused to acknowledge authorship for many years.

'Twas the night before Christmas, when all through the house
Not a creature was stirring, not even a mouse;
The stockings were hung by the chimney with care,
In hopes that Saint Nicholas soon would be there;

The children were nestled all snug in their beds,
While visions of sugar-plums danced in their heads;
And Mama in her 'kerchief, and I in my cap,
Had just settled our brains for a long winter's nap;

When out on the lawn there arose such a clatter,
I sprang from the bed to see what was the matter.
Away to the window I flew like a flash,
Tore open the shutters and threw up the sash.

The moon on the breast of the new-fallen snow
Gave the lustre of mid-day to objects below,
When what to my wondering sight should appear
But a miniature sleigh, and eight tiny reindeer,

With a little old driver, so lively and quick,
I knew in a moment it must be St. Nick.
More rapid than eagles his coursers they came,
And he whistled, and shouted, and called them by name:

"Now, *Dasher!* now, *Dancer!* now, *Prancer!* and *Vixen!*
On, *Comet!* on, *Cupid!* on, *Donner* and *Blitzen!*
To the top of the porch! To the top of the wall!
Now dash away! Dash away! Dash away all!"

As dry leaves that before the wild hurricane fly,
When they meet with an obstacle, mount to the sky,
So up to the house-top the coursers they flew,
With the sleigh full of toys, and St. Nicholas too.

And then, in a twinkling, I heard on the roof
The prancing and pawing of each little hoof –
As I drew in my head and was turning around,
Down the chimney St. Nicholas came with a bound.

He was dressed all in fur from his head to his foot,
And his clothes were all tarnished with ashes and soot;
A bundle of toys he had flung on his back,
And he looked like a peddler just opening his pack.

His eyes – how they sparkled! His dimples how merry!
His cheeks were like roses, his nose like a cherry!
His droll little mouth was drawn up like a bow,
And the beard of his chin was as white as the snow;

The stump of a pipe he held tight in his teeth,
And the smoke it encircled his head like a wreath;
He had a broad face and a little round belly,
That shook when he laughed like a bowlful of jelly.

He was chubby and plump, a right jolly old elf,
And I laughed when I saw him, in spite of myself;
A wink of his eye and a twist of his head
Soon gave me to know I had nothing to dread.

He spoke not a word but went straight to his work,
And filled all the stockings; then turned with a jerk,
And laying his finger aside of his nose,
And giving a nod, up the chimney he rose;

He sprang to his sleigh, to his team gave a whistle,
And away they all flew like the down of a thistle.
But I heard him exclaim, ere he drove out of sight,

'Happy Christmas to all,
And to all a good night!'

Clement C. Moore (1779–1863)

No room at the inn

*This celebrated passage, which appears at Luke 2:1–7, describes the humble
surroundings in which Jesus Christ was born. It tells how Joseph and Mary
were forced to travel to Bethlehem for registration but were refused a room at
the inn, so causing Christ to be laid in a manger. It forms an essential part of
carol services each Christmas. The phrase 'no room at the inn' has long since
entered the vernacular.*

In those days a decree went out from Emperor Augustus that all the
world should be registered. This was the first registration and was
taken while Quirinius was governor of Syria. All went to their own
towns to be registered. Joseph also went from the town of Nazareth
in Galilee to Judea, to the city of David called Bethlehem, because he
was descended from the house and family of David. He went to be
registered with Mary, to whom he was engaged and who was expecting
a child. While they were there, the time came for her to deliver her
child. And she gave birth to her firstborn son and wrapped him in
bands of cloth, and laid him in a manger, because there was no place
for them in the inn.

Now the holly bears a berry

This carol (sometimes called the St Day Carol) is a traditional English air.
The association of the Virgin Mary with holly (masculine) runs counter to the
usual identification of Mary with ivy (holly's feminine equivalent).

Now the holly bears a berry as white as the milk,
And Mary bore Jesus who was wrapped up in silk.

And Mary bore Jesus Christ, our Saviour for to be,
And the first tree of the greenwood, it was the holly;
Holly! holly!
And the first tree of the greenwood, it was the holly.

Now the holly bears a berry as black as a coal,
And Mary bore Jesus, who died for us all.

Now the holly bears a berry as red as the blood,
And Mary bore Jesus, who died on the Rood.

Anonymous (verse 4, W. D. Watson, dates unknown)

Now ys the time of Crystymas

*This plea in favour of festive jollity is of early sixteenth-century origin,
appearing in the* Commonplace Book of Richard Hill, *now preserved in
manuscript form in Balliol College, Oxford. Richard Hill compiled his book in
London, where he worked as a grocer.*

Make we mery both more and lasse,
For now ys the time of Crystymas.

Lett no man cum into this hall,
Grome, page, nor yet marshall,
But that sum sport he bring withal;
For now ys the tyme of Crystymas!

Yff that he say he can not sing,
Some oder sport then let him bring,
That yt may please at thys festyng;
For now ys the tyme of Crystymas!

Yff he say he can nowght do,
Then for my love aske hym no mo,
But to the stokkis then lett hym go;
For now ys the tyme of Crystymas!

Richard Hill (c.1490–1535)

O Christmas tree, O Christmas tree

This is a traditional German carol, also known by its German title
'O Tannenbaum'. Evergreens were important in pre-Christian pagan culture
and remain central in the imagery of Christmas today. German tradition
insists that the first Christmas trees were introduced by Martin Luther,
although it seems more likely that they were first included among the
Christmas festivities in late-medieval Rhineland, perhaps inspired by the
Tree of Life of the mystery plays.

O Christmas tree, O Christmas tree,
With faithful leaves unchanging!
Not only green in summer's heat
But in the winter's snow and sleet:
O Christmas tree, O Christmas tree,
With faithful leaves unchanging!

O Christmas tree, O Christmas tree,
Of all the trees most lovely!
Each year you bring renewed delight,
A-gleaming in the Christmas night:
O Christmas tree, O Christmas tree,
Of all the trees most lovely!

O Christmas tree, O Christmas tree,
Your leaves will surely trach me
That hope and love and faithfulness
Are precious things I can possess:
O Christmas tree, O Christmas tree,
Your leaves will surely teach me.

    Anonymous

O come, all ye faithful

John Francis Wade was a copier of manuscripts who is thought to have written these verses in 1744 while living at the Roman Catholic College for Englishmen at Douai in northern France. They were subsequently included in a packet of manuscripts sent to the English Roman Catholic College in Lisbon in 1750 but it was not until 1785 that they found their way back to England and, via the Portuguese chapel in London, began the process of becoming a worldwide favourite. Tradition has it that the final verse is sung only on Christmas Day.

O come, all ye faithful,
Joyful and triumphant,
O come ye, O come ye to Bethlehem:
Come and behold Him
Born the King of angels.

O come, let us adore Him,
O come, let us adore Him,
O come, let us adore Him,
Christ the Lord!

God of God,
Light of light,
Lo, He abhors not the virgin's womb;
Very God,
Begotten, not created.

See how the shepherds,
Summoned to His cradle,
Leaving their flocks, draw nigh with lowly fear;
We too will thither
Bend our joyful footsteps.

Lo, star-led chieftains,
Magi, Christ adoring,
Offer Him incense, gold and myrrh;
We to the Christ-child
Bring our hearts' oblations.

Child, for us sinners,
Poor and in the manger,
Fain we embrace Thee with love and awe;
Who would not love Thee,
Loving us so dearly?

Sing, choirs of angels,
Sing in exultation,
Sing, all ye citizens of heaven above,
'Glory to God
In the highest'.

Yea, Lord, we greet Thee,
Born this happy morning,
Jesu, to Thee be all glory given;
Word of the Father,
Now in flesh appearing.

John Francis Wade (1711–86), adapted by
Frederick Oakley (1802–80) and others

O come, O come, Emmanuel

This popular carol was written by an unidentified German hymn writer in the early eighteenth century. It appears to have been inspired by the brief verses called antiphons, sung each day during Advent as far back as the ninth century. During Advent, these antiphons celebrating the coming of Christ (each beginning with 'O', and thus known as the 'Great Os of Advent') were sung by high-ranking monks of medieval monasteries. These monks were allotted one antiphon each and had to 'pay' for this privilege by providing hospitality for all present when they sang their verse. The modern hymn was created from these antiphons being strung together. The tune is thought to date from the thirteenth century.

O come, O come, Emmanuel,
And ransom captive Israel,
That mourns in lonely exile here
Until the Son of God appear.

Rejoice! Rejoice! Emmanuel
Shall come to thee, O Israel.

O come, thou Wisdom from above
Who orderest all things through Thy love;
To us the path of knowledge show
And teach us in her ways to go.

O come, O come, thou Lord of might,
Who to Thy tribes, on Sinai's height,
In ancient times didst give the law
In cloud, and majesty, and awe.

O come, thou Rod of Jesse, free
Thine own from Satan's tyranny;
From depths of hell Thy people save,
And give them victory o'er the grave.

O come, thou Key of David, come
And open wide our heavenly home;
Make safe the way that leads on high,
And close the path to misery.

O come, thou Dayspring, come and cheer
Our spirits by Thine advent here;
Disperse the gloomy clouds of night,
And death's dark shadows put to flight.

O come, Desire of nations, bring
All peoples to their Saviour King;
Thou Corner-stone, who makest one,
Complete in us Thy work begun.

Anonymous, translated by John Mason Neale (1818–66)

O holy night

Placide Cappeau, the author of this French carol (otherwise known as 'Cantique de Noël'), was a wine merchant and occasional poet who was invited to compose a Christmas poem by the local priest in his home town of Roquemaure. The lines were set to music by the Parisian composer Adolphe Adam (1803–56) and the carol was first performed on Christmas Eve 1847. It is remembered as the carol sung by French soldiers to their German opponents in the trenches outside Paris during the Franco-Prussian War (1870–71). The Germans responded by singing 'From Heaven above to earth I come'.

O holy night, the stars are brightly shining,
It is the night of the dear Saviour's birth;
Long lay the world in sin and error pining,
Till He appeared and the soul felt it's worth.
A thrill of hope the weary soul rejoices,
For yonder breaks a new and glorious morn.

Fall on your knees, Oh hear the angel voices!
O night divine, O night when Christ was born!
O night divine, O holy night, O night divine.

Led by the light of Faith serenely beaming
With glowing hearts by His cradle we stand
So led by light of a star sweetly gleaming
Here come the wise men from Orient land
The King of Kings lay thus in lowly manger
In all our trials born to be our friend.

Truly He taught us to love one another
His law is love and His gospel is peace
Chains shall He break for the slave is our brother
And in His name all oppression shall cease
Sweet hymns of joy in grateful chorus raise we,
Let all within us praise His holy name.

Placide Cappeau (1808–77), translated by
John Sullivan Dwight (1812–93)

O little town of Bethlehem

Phillips Brooks, an American preacher in Philadelphia, was inspired to write this enduringly popular Christmas carol after going on a pilgrimage to the Holy Land in 1865. He composed these verses after visiting the field outside Bethlehem where the shepherds are supposed to have experienced the annunciation.

O little town of Bethlehem,
How still we see thee lie!
Above thy deep and dreamless sleep
The silent stars go by.
Yet in thy dark streets shineth
The everlasting light;
The hopes and fears of all the years
Are met in thee tonight.

O morning stars, together
Proclaim the holy birth
And praises sing to God the King,
And peace to all the earth.
For Christ is born of Mary;
And, gathered all above,
While mortals sleep, the angels keep
Their watch of wondering love.

How silently, how silently,
The wondrous gift is given!
So God imparts to human hearts
The blessings of His heaven.
No ear may hear His coming;
But in this world of sin,
Where meek souls will receive Him, still
The dear Christ enters in.

Where children pure and happy
Pray to the blessed child,
Where misery cries out to Thee,
Son of the mother mild;
Where charity stands watching
And faith holds wide the door,
The dark night wakes, the glory breaks,
And Christmas comes once more.

O Holy Child of Bethlehem,
Descend to us, we pray;
Cast out our sin, and enter in,
Be born in us today.
We hear the Christmas angels
The great glad tidings tell:
O come to us, abide with us,
Our Lord, Emmanuel.

Phillips Brooks (1835–93)

Of the Father's heart begotten

This Christmas hymn (entitled in Latin 'Corde natus ex parentis') is attributed to the Romano-Spanish lawyer and poet Aurelius Clemens Prudentius. Prudentius subsequently gave up his secular career, which included the post of head of the bodyguard to Emperor Honorius, in order to dedicate himself to spiritual contemplation in a monastery. The tune to which the hymn is sung is medieval.

Of the Father's love begotten
Ere the worlds began to be,
He is Alpha and Omega,
He the source, the ending He,
Of the things that are, that have been,
And that future years shall see,
Evermore and evermore.

At His word was all created;
He commanded, it was done:
Earth, and heaven, and depths of ocean,
In their threefold order one;
All that grows beneath the shining
Of the orbs of moon and sun
Evermore and evermore.

He assumed this mortal body,
Frail and feeble, doomed to die,
That the race from dust created
Might not perish utterly,
Which the dreadful Law had sentenced
In the depths of hell to lie
Evermore and evermore.

O that birth, for ever blessed!
When the Virgin, full of grace,
By the Holy Ghost conceiving,
Bore the Saviour of our race,
And the Child, the world's Redeemer,
First revealed His sacred face
Evermore and evermore.

O ye heights of heaven, adore him!
Angel-hosts, his praises sing!
Powers, dominions, bow before Him,
And extol your God and King!
Let no tongue today be silent,
Every voice in concert ring
Evermore and evermore.

This is He whom once the sibyls
With united voice foretold,
His the birth that faithful prophets
In their pages did unfold;
Let the world unite to praise him,
Long-desired, foreseen of old
Evermore and evermore.

Hail, Thou Judge of souls departed!
Hail, Thou King of them that thrive!
On the Father's throne exalted
None in might with Thee may strive,
Who at last, to judge returning,
Sinners from Thy face shall drive
Evermore and evermore.

O ye elders, lead the anthems:
Laud your God in ancient lays!
Youths and maidens, hymn his glory!
Infants, bring your songs of praise!
Guileless voices, in sweet concord
Unto all the length of days
Evermore and evermore.

Let the storm and summer sunshine,
Gliding stream and sounding shore,
Sea and forest, frost and zephyr,
Night and day their Lord adore;
All Creation joined to praise Thee
Through the ages evermore
Evermore and evermore.

Christ, to Thee, with God the Father,
And, O Holy Ghost, to Thee,
High thanksgiving, endless praises,
And eternal glory be;
Honour, power, and all dominion,
And eternal victory
Evermore and evermore.

Aurelius Clemens Prudentius (348–413), adapted by
John Mason Neale (1818–66) and Roby Furley Davis (1866–1937)

Old Sam's Christmas pudding

These lines became widely familiar as a comic monologue performed by the comedian Stanley Holloway (1890–1982). Christmas puddings have inspired numerous songs and poems, but none experienced anything to parallel the adventures of this particular example.

It was Christmas Day in the trenches
In Spain in Peninsular War,
And Sam Small were cleaning his musket
A thing as he ne'er done before.

They'd had 'em inspected that morning,
And Sam had got into disgrace
For when Sergeant had looked down the barrel
A sparrow flew out in his face.

The Sergeant reported the matter
To Lieutenant Bird then and there.
Said Lieutenant 'How very disgusting
The Duke must be told of this 'ere.'

The Duke were upset when he heard,
He said 'I'm astonished, I am.
I must make a most drastic example
There'll be no Christmas pudding for Sam.'

When Sam were informed of his sentence
Surprise rooted him to the spot –
'Twere much worse than he had expected,
He thought as he'd only be shot.

And so he sat cleaning his musket,
And polishing barrel and butt,
Whilst the pudding his mother had sent him
Lay there in the mud at his foot.

Now the centre that Sam's lot were holding
Ran around a place called Badajoz
Where the Spaniards had put up a bastion
And ooh what a bastion it was!

They pounded away all the morning
With canister, grape shot and ball,
But the face of the bastion defied them
They made no impression at all.

They started again after dinner
Bombarding as hard as they could;
And the Duke brought his own private cannon
But that weren't a ha'pence o' good.

The Duke said 'Sam, put down thy musket
And help me to lay this gun true.'
Sam answered 'You'd best ask your favours
From them as you give pudding to.'

The Duke looked at Sam so reproachful
'And don't take it that way,' said he,
'Us Generals have got to be ruthless
It hurts me more than it did thee.'

Sam sniffed at these words kind of sceptic,
Then looked down the Duke's private gun
And said 'We'd best put in two charges
We'll never bust bastion with one.'

He tipped cannon ball out of muzzle,
He took out the wadding and all,
He filled barrel chock full of powder,
Then picked up and replaced the ball.

He took a good aim at the bastion
Then said 'Right-o, Duke, let her fly.'
The cannon nigh jumped off her trunnions
And up went the bastion, sky high.

The Duke he weren't 'alf elated,
He danced round the trench full of glee
And said 'Sam, for this gallant action
You can hot up your pudding for tea.'

Sam looked round to pick up his pudding.
But it wasn't there, nowhere about.
In the place where he thought he had left it
Lay the cannon ball he'd just tipped out.

Sam saw in a flash what 'ad happened:
By an unprecedented mishap
The pudding his mother had sent him
Had blown Badajoz off the map.

That's why Fusilliers wear to this moment
A badge which they think's a grenade,
But they're wrong – it's a brass reproduction
Of the pudding Sam's mother once made.

Marriott Edgar (1880–1951)

Permission has been sought.

On a winter's night long time ago

The French-born Anglophile Hilaire Belloc was well-known as an enthusiastic Roman Catholic apologist. In this poem he presents his own vision of the events of the first Christmas Eve.

On a winter's night long time ago
(The bells ring loud and the bells ring low)
When high howled wind, and down fell snow,
(Carillon, Carilla)
Saint Joseph he and Nostre Dame,
Riding on an ass, full weary came
From Nazareth into Bethlehem.
And the small child Jesus smile on you.

And Bethlehem inn they stood before
(The bells ring less and the bells ring more)
The landlord bade them begone from his door,
(Carillon, Carilla)
'Poor folk' (says he) 'must lie where they may,
For the Duke of Jewry comes this way,
With all his train on a Christmas Day.'
And the small child Jesus smile on you.

Poor folk that may my carol hear
(The bells ring single and the bells ring clear)
See! God's one child had hardest cheer!
(Carillon, Carilla)
Men grown hard on a Christmas morn:
The dumb beast by and a babe forlorn,
It was very, very cold when Our Lord was born.
And the small child Jesus smile on you.

Now these were Jews as Jews must be
(The bells ring merry and the bells ring free)
But Christian men in a band are we
(Carillon, Carilla).
Empty we go, and ill be-dight,
Singing Noël on a winter's night:
Give us to sup by the warm firelight,
And the small child Jesus smile on you.

Hilaire Belloc (1870–1953)

Permission has been sought.

On Christmas night all Christians sing

This popular carol (also known as 'The Sussex carol') evolved from an earlier carol written by the Irish Franciscan Bishop Luke Wadding in the seventeenth century. It was subsequently collected by the composer Vaughan Williams from one of his singers, Mrs Verrall, who came from Sussex. Vaughan Williams wrote the arrangement to which these lines are sung today.

On Christmas night all Christians sing,
To hear the news the angels bring.
News of great joy, news of great mirth,
News of our merciful King's birth.

Then why should men on earth be so sad,
Since our Redeemer made us glad
When from our sin he set us free,
All for to gain our liberty?

When sin departs before his grace,
Then life and health come in its place;
Angels and men with joy may sing,
All for to see the new-born King.

All out of darkness we have light,
Which made the angels sing this night:
'Glory to God and peace to men,
Now and for evermore. Amen.'

Anonymous, after Bishop Luke Wadding (d.1686)

Once in royal David's city

Cecil Frances Alexander was a minister's wife who dedicated herself to work on behalf of the 'poor, and mean, and lonely' in her husband's parish. She was also the author of such celebrated hymns as 'All things bright and beautiful' and 'There is a green hill far away'. Her famous carol is traditionally sung by a lone choirboy at the beginning of the Service of Nine Lessons and Carols broadcast on Christmas Eve each year from King's College, Cambridge. For many people this moment marks the beginning of the Christmas festivities.

Once in royal David's city
Stood a lowly cattle shed,
Where a mother laid her baby,
In a manger for His bed.
Mary was that mother mild,
Jesus Christ her little Child.

He came down to earth from heaven
Who is God and Lord of all,
And His shelter was a stable,
And His cradle was a stall.
With the poor, and mean, and lowly
Lived on earth, our Saviour holy.

And through all His wondrous childhood
He would honour and obey,
Love, and watch the lowly mother
In whose gentle arms He lay.
Christian children all must be
Mild, obedient, good as He.

For He is our childhood's pattern:
Day by day like us He grew;
He was little, weak, and helpless;
Tears and smiles like us He knew;
And He feeleth for our sadness,
And He shareth in our gladness.

And our eyes at last shall see Him,
Through His own redeeming love;
For that child so dear and gentle
Is our Lord in heav'n above;
And He leads His children on
To the place where He is gone.

Not in that poor lowly stable,
With the oxen standing round,
We shall see Him, but in heaven,
Set at God's right hand on high,
When, like stars, His children crowned,
All in white shall wait around.

Cecil Frances Alexander (1818–95)

Out of Bethlehem

These words, from Micah 5:2–5, comprise a prophecy about the future birth of Christ in Bethlehem. They are sometimes selected for readings during the Christmas period.

But you, O Bethlehem of Ephrathah, who are one of the little clans of Judah, from you shall come forth for me one who is to rule in Israel, whose origin is from of old, from ancient days. Therefore he shall give them up until the time when she who is in labour has brought forth; then the rest of his kindred shall return to the people of Israel. And he shall stand and feed his flock in the strength of the LORD, in the majesty of the name of the LORD his God. And they shall live secure, for now he shall be great to the ends of the earth; and he shall be the one of peace.

Out of Jacob

This passage, from Numbers 24:15–19, foretells the coming of Christ as the Saviour of his people. The star that comes out of Jacob refers ultimately to Christ himself, for he describes himself as 'the bright morning star' (Revelation 22:16). The sceptre is a symbol of kingship. Jacob was the respected patriarch and the ancestor of the twelve tribes of Israel.

So he uttered his oracle, saying: 'The oracle of Balaam son of Beor, the oracle of the man whose eye is clear, the oracle of one who hears the words of God, and knows the knowledge of the Most High, who sees the vision of the Almighty, who falls down, but with his eyes uncovered: I see him, but not now; I behold him, but not near – a star shall come out of Jacob, and a sceptre shall rise out of Israel; it shall crush the borderlands of Moab, and the territory of all the Shethites. Edom will become a possession, Seir a possession of its enemies, while Israel does valiantly. One out of Jacob shall rule, and destroy the survivors of Ir.'

A Pepysian Christmas

This entry from Pepys's diary, written on 25 December 1662, furnishes the reader with various details of Christmas as it was celebrated at Court in Restoration England.

Had a pleasant walk to White Hall, where I intended to have received the Communion with the family, but I come a little too late. So I walked up into the house, and spent my time in looking over pictures, particularly the ships in King Henry the VIIIth's voyage to Bullaen; marking the great difference between those built then and now. By and by down the chapel again, where Bishop Morley preached upon the song of the Angels, 'Glory to God on high, on earth peace, and good will towards men.' Methought he made but a poor sermon, but long, and reprehending the common jollity of the Court for the true joy that shall and ought to be on these days, he particularized concerning their excess in playes and gaming, saying that he whose office it is to keep the gamesters in order and within bounds, serves but for a second rather in a duell, meaning the groome-porter. Upon which it was worth observing how far they are come from taking the reprehensions of a bishop seriously, that they all laugh in the chapel when he reflected on their ill actions and courses. He did much press us to joy in these public days of joy, and to hospitality; but one that stood by whispered in my eare that the Bishop do not spend one groate to the poore himself. The sermon done, a good anthem followed with vialls, and the King come down to receive the Sacrament. But I staid not, but calling my boy from my Lord's lodgings, and giving Sarah some good advice by my Lord's order to be sober, and look after the house, I walked home again with great pleasure, and there dined by my wife's bed-side with great content, having a mess of brave plum-porridge and a roasted pullet for dinner, and I sent for a mince-pie abroad, my wife not being well, to make any herself yet.

Samuel Pepys (1633–1703)

Personent hodie

This carol is unusual, being equally familiar in both its Latin and English versions. It is thought to have been composed for the choirboys' feast held in various cathedrals on Holy Innocents' Day, when the choristers and their masters exchanged roles and privileges. The usual musical arrangement was contributed by the composer Gustav Holst (1874–1934).

Latin:
Personent hodie
Voces puerulae
Laudantes iucunde
Qui nobis est natus,
Summo Deo datus,
Et de virgineo
Ventre procreatus.

In mundo nascitur;
Pannis involvitur;
Praesepi ponitur
Stabulo brutorum
Rector supernorum;
Perdidit spolia
Pinceps Infernorum.

Magi tres venerunt;
Munera offerunt;
Parvulum inquirunt,
Stellulam sequendo,
Ipsum adorando,
Aurum, thus et myrrham
Ei offerendo.

Omnes clericuli,
Pariter pueri,
Cantent ut angeli:
'Advenisti mundo:
Laudes tibi fundo
Ideo: Gloria
In excelsis Deo.'

English:
On this day earth shall ring
With the song children sing
To the Son, Christ the King,
Born on earth to save us;
Him the Father gave us.
Ideo Gloria in excelsis Deo!

His the doom, ours the mirth,
When he came down to earth;
Bethlehem saw his birth;
Ox and ass, beside him,
From the cold would hide him.
Ideo Gloria in excelsis Deo!

God's bright star, o'er his head,
Wise men three to him led;
Kneel they low by his bed,
Lay their gifts before him,
Praise him and adore him.
Ideo Gloria in excelsis Deo!

On this day angels sing;
With their song earth shall ring,
Praising Christ, heaven's King,
Born on earth to save us;
Peace and love he gave us.
Ideo Gloria in excelsis Deo!

Anonymous, adapted by Jane M. Joseph (1894–1929)

The Pickwick Papers

This description of Christmas jollity comes from The Pickwick Papers *by Charles Dickens. It remains one of the best-loved evocations of festive merrymaking.*

From the centre of the ceiling of this kitchen, old Wardle had just suspended, with his own hands, a huge branch of mistletoe, and this same branch of mistletoe instantaneously gave rise to a scene of general and most delightful struggling and confusion; in the midst of which, Mr Pickwick, with a gallantry that would have done honour to a descendant of Lady Tollimglower herself, took the old lady by the hand, led her beneath the mystic branch, and saluted her in all courtesy and decorum. The old lady submitted to this piece of practical politeness with all the dignity which befitted so important and serious a solemnity, but the younger ladies, not being so thoroughly imbued with a superstitious veneration for the custom: or imagining that the value of a salute is very much enhanced if it cost a little trouble to obtain it: screamed and struggled, and ran into corners, and threatened and remonstrated, and did everything but leave the room, until some of the less adventurous gentlemen were on the point of desisting, when they all at once found it useless to resist any longer, and submitted to be kissed with a good grace. Mr Winkle kissed the young lady with the black eyes, and Mr Snodgrass kissed Emily, and Mr Weller, not being particular about the form of being under the mistletoe, kissed Emma and the other female servants, just as he caught them. As to the poor relations, they kissed everybody, not even excepting the plainer portions of the young-lady visitors, who, in their excessive confusion, ran right under the mistletoe, as soon as it was hung up, without knowing it! Wardle stood with his back to the fire, surveying the whole scene, with the utmost satisfaction; and the fat boy took the opportunity of appropriating to his own use, and summarily devouring, a particularly fine mince-pie, that had been carefully put by, for somebody else.

Now, the screaming had subsided, and faces were in a glow, and curls in a tangle, and Mr Pickwick, after kissing the old lady as before mentioned, was standing under the mistletoe, looking with a very pleased countenance on all that was passing around him, when the young lady with the black eyes, after a little whispering with the other young ladies, made a sudden dart forward, and, putting her arm round

Mr Pickwick's neck, saluted him affectionately on the left cheek; and before Mr Pickwick distinctly knew what was the matter, he was surrounded by the whole body, and kissed by every one of them.

It was a pleasant thing to see Mr Pickwick in the centre of the group, now pulled this way, and then that, and first kissed on the chin, and then on the nose, and then on the spectacles: and to hear the peals of laughter which were raised on every side; but it was a still more pleasant thing to see Mr Pickwick, blinded shortly afterwards with a silk handkerchief, falling up against the wall, and scrambling into corners, and going through all the mysteries of blind-man's buff, with the utmost relish for the game, until at last he caught one of the poor relations, and then had to evade the blind-man himself, which he did with a nimbleness and agility that elicited the admiration and applause of all beholders. The poor relations caught the people who they thought would like it, and, when the game flagged, got caught themselves. When they were all tired of blind-man's buff, there was a great game at snap-dragon, and when fingers enough were burned with that, and all the raisins were gone, they sat down by the huge fire of blazing logs to a substantial supper, and a mighty bowl of wassail, something smaller than an ordinary wash-house copper, in which the hot apples were hissing and bubbling with a rich look, and a jolly sound, that were perfectly irresistible.

'This,' said Mr Pickwick, looking round him, 'this is, indeed, comfort.'

Charles Dickens (1812–70)

A Puritan Christmas

This entry, dated 25 December 1657, comes from the diary of English writer John Evelyn. It vividly portrays the risks involved in celebrating Christmas after such festivities were prohibited by the Puritan authorities in the years prior to the Restoration of 1660.

I went to London with my wife, to celebrate Christmas-day, Mr. Gunning preaching in Exeter-Chapell, on 7 Micah 2. Sermon ended, as he was giving us the holy sacrament, the chapel was surrounded with souldiers, and all the communicants and assembly surpriz'd and kept prisoners by them, some in the house, others carried away. It fell to my share to be confin'd to a room in the house, where yet I was permitted to dine with the master of it, the Countess of Dorset, Lady Hatton, and some others of quality who invited me. In the afternoone came Col. Whaly, Goffe, and others, from White-hall, to examine us one by one; some they committed to the Marshall, some to prison. When I came before them they took my name and abode, examin'd me why, contrarie to an ordinance made that none should any longer observe the superstitious time of the Nativity (so esteem'd by them) I durst offend, and particularly be at Common Prayers, which they told me was but the Masse in English, and particularly pray for Charles Steuart, for which we had no Scripture. I told them we did not pray for Cha. Stewart, but for all Christian Kings, Princes, and Governours. They replied, in so doing we praid for the K. of Spaine too, who was their enemie and a papist, with other frivolous and insnaring questions and much threatening: and finding no colour to detaine me, they dismiss'd me with much pitty of my ignorance. These were men of high flight and above ordinances, and spake spiteful things of our Lord's Nativity. As we went up to receive the sacrament the miscreants held their muskets against us as if they would have shot us at the altar, but yet suffering us to finish the office of Communion, as perhaps not having instructions what to do in case they found us in that action. So I got home late the next day, blessed by God.

John Evelyn (1620–1706)

Rejoice, ye tenants of the earth

This carol is well-known by virtue of its appearance in the Thomas Hardy novel Under the Greenwood Tree (1872), *in which it is sung by the Mellstock choir. Hardy knew it as one of the carols performed by the carol party in which his own father participated.*

Rejoice, ye tenants of the earth,
And celebrate your Saviour's birth!
This is the happy morn,
On which the angels did impart
These tidings to each longing heart:
'Your Saviour, Christ, is born!'

Behold! a meteor, shining bright,
Conducts the eastern sages right
To Judah's distant land,
And guides to Bethlehem their road,
Then fixes o'er his low abode,
Directed by his hand.

And here they find the new-born King,
To whom they did their offerings bring
And worship at his feet,
While angels, flying from their home,
Proclaim that he alone is come,
Salvation to complete.

For us these acclamations fly,
For us he's born, below to die,
That he may reign above:
Then let us all our voices raise
And sound abroad our Saviour's praise
For his unbounded love.

William Gifford (c.1738–1809)

Rocking carol

This carol is of Czech origin and was collected (under the title 'Hajej, nynej, Jezisku') in the early 1920s. Clergyman and socialist Percy Dearmer translated the carol into English for the Oxford Book of Carols in 1928. It is thought that the carol was sung originally to the rocking of a baby's cradle. It became widely known in the English-speaking world following the release of a recording of the carol by actress and singer Julie Andrews.

Little Jesus, sweetly sleep, do not stir;
We will lend a coat of fur,
We will rock you, rock you, rock you,
We will rock you, rock you, rock you:
See the fur to keep you warm,
Snugly round your tiny form.

Mary's little baby, sleep, sweetly sleep,
Sleep in comfort, slumber deep;
We will rock you, rock you, rock you,
We will rock you, rock you, rock you:
We will serve you all we can,
Darling, darling little man.

Anonymous, translated by Percy Dearmer (1867–1936)

The rod of Jesse

This passage from Isaiah 11:1–9 is one of the most famous biblical expressions of peace, justice and reconciliation. This makes it a popular choice of reading during the 'season of peace and goodwill'.

A shoot shall come out from the stock of Jesse, and a branch shall grow out of his roots. The spirit of the LORD shall rest on him, the spirit of wisdom and understanding, the spirit of counsel and might, the spirit of knowledge and the fear of the LORD. His delight shall be in the fear of the LORD.

He shall not judge by what his eyes see, or decide by what his ears hear; but with righteousness he shall judge the poor, and decide with equity for the meek of the earth; he shall strike the earth with the rod of his mouth, and with the breath of his lips he shall kill the wicked. Righteousness shall be the belt around his waist, and faithfulness the belt around his loins.

The wolf shall live with the lamb, the leopard shall lie down with the kid, the calf and the lion and the fatling together, and a little child shall lead them. The cow and the bear shall graze, their young shall lie down together; and the lion shall eat straw like the ox. The nursing child shall play over the hole of the asp, and the weaned child shall put its hand on the adder's den. They will not hurt or destroy on all my holy mountain; for the earth will be full of the knowledge of the LORD as the waters cover the sea.

Rudolph the red-nosed reindeer

This very familiar Christmas song was originally a poem written by an American advertising executive called Robert L. May. He wrote these verses in 1939 as a free gift for Father Christmas to give to children visiting him in a Chicago department store. Such was the appeal of the poem that almost 2.5 million copies of the poem were handed out over that first Christmas. The poem is most familiar today as a song, as recorded in 1949 by singer Gene Autry to a tune by Johnny Marks.

Rudolph, the red-nosed reindeer
Had a very shiny nose.
And if you ever saw him,
You would even say it glows.

All of the other reindeer
Used to laugh and call him names.
They never let poor Rudolph
Join in any reindeer games.

Then one foggy Christmas Eve
Santa came to say:
'Rudolph with your nose so bright,
Won't you guide my sleigh tonight?'

Then all the reindeer loved him
As they shouted out with glee,
Rudolph the red-nosed reindeer,
You'll go down in history!

Robert L. May (b.1906)

Permission has been sought.

Saint Stephen and King Herod

*The story of the martyrdom of Saint Stephen tends to be overshadowed by
the festivities surrounding the birth of Christ, largely because the Feast of
St Stephen falls on 26 December, immediately after Christmas Day. This
old English ballad relates what happened, and makes clear the connection
between Saint Stephen's death and Christ's birth.*

Saint Stephen was a clerk
In King Herod's hall,
And served him of bread and cloth
As every king befall.

Stephen out of kitchen came
With boar's head on hand,
He saw a star was fair and bright
Over Bethlehem stand.

He cast adown the boar's head
And went into the hall;
'I forsake thee, Herod,
And thy workes all.

'I forsake thee, King Herod,
And thy workes all,
There is a child in Bethlehem born
Is better than we all.'

'What aileth thee, Stephen?
What is thee befall?
Lacketh thee either meat or drink
In King Herod's hall?'

'Lacketh me neither meat or drink
In King Herod's hall;
There is a child in Bethlehem born
Is better than we all.'

'What aileth thee Stephen?
Art wode or 'ginnest to brede?
Lacketh thee either gold or fee,
Or any rich weed?'

'Lacketh me neither gold ne fee
Ne none rich weed;
There is a child in Bethlehem born
Shall helpen us at our need.'

'That is all so sooth, Stephen,
All so sooth, I-wys,
As this capon crowe shall
That li'th here in my dish.'

That word was not so soon said,
That word in that hall,
The capon crew Christus natus est
Among the lordes all.

'Risit up, my tormentors,
By two and all by one,
And leadit Stephen out of this town,
And stonit him with stone.'

Tooken they Stephen
And stoned him in the way;
And therefore is his even
On Christe's own day.

Anonymous

See, amid the winter's snow

This carol was written by an Anglican priest who was among those to follow the example of John Henry Newman in turning to Roman Catholicism. He composed this carol, which was first published in 1851, shortly after his conversion.

See, amid the winter's snow,
Born for us on earth below,
See, the tender Lamb appears,
Promised from eternal years!

Hail, thou ever-blessed morn!
Hail, Redemption's happy dawn!
Sing through all Jerusalem:
'Christ is born in Bethlehem!'

Lo! within a manger lies
He who built the starry skies,
He who, throned in height sublime,
Sits amid the Cherubim.

Say, ye holy shepherds, say:
What your joyful news today?
Wherefore have ye left your sheep
On the lonely mountain steep?

As we watched at dead of night,
Lo! we saw a wondrous light;
Angels, singing 'Peace on earth',
Told us of the Saviour's birth.

Sacred Infant, all-divine,
What a tender love was Thine
Thus to come from highest bliss
Down to such a world as this!

Teach, oh teach us, holy Child,
By Thy face so meek and mild,
Teach us to resemble Thee
In Thy sweet humility!

Edward Caswall (1814–78)

A Shavian Christmas

This humorous indictment of the Christmas season appeared in The World *on 23 December 1893. Even in Shaw's time, many railed against the evident commercialisation of Christmas and lamented the extent to which its religious meaning was being forgotten (though Shaw himself was no defender of the Church).*

Like all intelligent people, I greatly dislike Christmas. It revolts me to see a whole nation refrain from music for weeks together in order that every man may rifle his neighbour's pockets under cover of a ghastly general pretence of festivity. It is really an atrocious institution, this Christmas. We must be gluttonous because it is Christmas. We must be drunken because it is Christmas. We must be insincerely generous; we must buy things that nobody wants, and give them to people we don't like; we must go to absurd entertainments that make even our little children satirical; we must writhe under venal officiousness from legions of freebooters, all because it is Christmas – that is, because the mass of the population, including the all-powerful middle-class tradesman, depends on a week of licence and brigandage, waste and intemperance, to clear off its outstanding liabilities at the end of the year. As for me, I shall fly from it all tomorrow or next day to some remote spot miles from a shop, where nothing worse can befall me than a serenade from a few peasants, or some equally harmless survival of medieval mummery, shyly proffered, not advertised, moderate in its expectations, and soon over. In town there is, for the moment, nothing for me or any honest man to do.

George Bernard Shaw (1856–1950)

The Society of Authors, on behalf of the Bernard Shaw Estate.
Reproduced with permission.

The shepherds and the angels

This passage from Luke 2:8–20 describes how the shepherds were told by an angel about the birth of Christ. The shepherds then went quickly to find Mary, Joseph and the baby. Their encounter with God led them to tell others and to worship God deeply for themselves.

In that region there were shepherds living in the fields, keeping watch over their flock by night. Then an angel of the Lord stood before them, and the glory of the Lord shone around them, and they were terrified. But the angel said to them, 'Do not be afraid; for see – I am bringing you good news of great joy for all the people: to you is born this day in the city of David a Saviour, who is the Messiah, the Lord. This will be a sign for you: you will find a child wrapped in bands of cloth and lying in a manger.' And suddenly there was with the angel a multitude of the heavenly host, praising God and saying, 'Glory to God in the highest heaven, and on earth peace among those whom he favours!'

When the angels had left them and gone into heaven, the shepherds said to one another, 'Let us go now to Bethlehem and see this thing that has taken place, which the Lord has made known to us.' So they went with haste and found Mary and Joseph, and the child lying in the manger. When they saw this, they made known what had been told them about this child; and all who heard it were amazed at what the shepherds told them. But Mary treasured all these words and pondered them in her heart. The shepherds returned, glorifying and praising God for all they had heard and seen, as it had been told them.

Silent night

This enduringly popular carol was written (so the story goes) because the church organ in the Austrian village of Unterweisburg had broken down just before Christmas 1818. So that the congregation would still have something to sing, the village's young curate Joseph Mohr rapidly composed some seasonal verses and invited Franz Grüber, the assistant organist, to set them to a simple guitar accompaniment. The carol was first performed at St Nicholas Church in Unterweisburg on Christmas Eve. Translated into English by John Freeman Young (1820–85), the carol was famously sung in the trenches by opposing British and German troops at Christmas 1914.

Silent night, holy night,
All is calm, all is bright
Round yon virgin mother and Child.
Holy Infant so tender and mild,
Sleep in heavenly peace,
Sleep in heavenly peace.

Silent night, holy night,
Shepherds quake at the sight.
Glories stream from heaven afar,
Heavenly hosts sing alleluia;
Christ the Saviour is born!
Christ the Saviour is born!

Silent night, holy night,
Son of God, love's pure light
Radiant beams from Thy holy face,
With the dawn of redeeming grace,
Jesus, Lord, at Thy birth,
Jesus, Lord, at Thy birth.

Joseph Mohr (1792–1848)

Simeon and Anna

This passage, from Luke 2:25–38, gives a rare glimpse into the early life of
Christ and so is occasionally read during the Christmas period. We read about
what happened to Simeon and Anna, two individuals who worshipped God.
Mary and Joseph are given confirmation of Jesus' special significance and
Mary is warned of the heartache to come.

Now there was a man in Jerusalem whose name was Simeon; this man
was righteous and devout, looking forward to the consolation of Israel,
and the Holy Spirit rested on him. It had been revealed to him by the
Holy Spirit that he would not see death before he had seen the Lord's
Messiah. Guided by the Spirit, Simeon came into the temple; and
when the parents brought in the child Jesus, to do for him what was
customary under the law, Simeon took him in his arms and praised
God, saying, 'Master, now you are dismissing your servant in peace,
according to your word; for my eyes have seen your salvation, which
you have prepared in the presence of all peoples, a light for revelation
to the Gentiles and for glory to your people Israel.'

And the child's father and mother were amazed at what was being
said about him. Then Simeon blessed them and said to his mother
Mary, 'This child is destined for the falling and the rising of many in
Israel, and to be a sign that will be opposed so that the inner thoughts
of many will be revealed – and a sword will pierce your own soul too.'

There was also a prophet, Anna the daughter of Phanuel, of the
tribe of Asher. She was of a great age, having lived with her husband for
seven years after her marriage, then as a widow to the age of eighty-
four. She never left the temple but worshipped there with fasting and
prayer night and day. At that moment she came, and began to praise
God and to speak about the child to all who were looking for the
redemption of Jerusalem.

Sir Roger de Coverley's Christmas

Sir Roger de Coverley was the fictional old country gentleman whose often comical opinions of the world were reported in the form of letters from the otherwise unidentified 'L' published in the Spectator *in the years 1711–12. 'L' was in fact the essayist Joseph Addison. Here L relates what Sir Roger has told him of the Christmas he has just passed.*

He afterwards fell into an Account of the Diversions which had passed in his House during the Holidays; for Sir Roger, after the laudable Custom of his Ancestors, always keeps open House at Christmas. I learned from him that he had killed eight Fat Hogs for this Season, that he had dealt about his Chines very liberally amongst his Neighbours, and that in particular he had sent a String of Hogs'-puddings with a Pack of Cards to every poor Family in the Parish. I have often thought, says Sir Roger, it happens very well that Christmas should fall out in the Middle of Winter. It is the most dead uncomfortable Time of the Year, when the poor People would suffer very much from their Poverty and Cold, if they had not good Chear, warm fires, and Christmas Gambols to support them. I love to rejoice their poor Hearts at this Season, and to see the whole Village merry in my great Hall. I allow a double Quantity of Malt to my Small Beer, and set it a-running for twelve Days to every one that calls for it. I have always a Piece of Cold Beef and Mince-pye upon the Table, and am wonderfully pleased to see my Tenants pass away a whole evening in playing their innocent Tricks, and smutting one another. Our Friend Will Wimble is as merry as any of them, and shews a thousand Roguish Tricks upon these Occasions.

I was very much delighted with the Reflexion of my old Friend, which carried so much Goodness with it. He then launched out into the Praise of the late Act of Parliament for securing the Church of England, and told me with great Satisfaction, that he believed it already began to take Effect, for that a rigid Dissenter who chanced to dine at his House on Christmas-day, had been observed to eat away very plentifully of his Plumb-porridge.

Joseph Addison (1672–1719)

Somehow not only for Christmas

In this poem John Greenleaf Whittier reminds the reader that generosity towards others is not something that should be reserved for Christmas alone.

Somehow not only for Christmas
But all the long year through,
The joy that you give to others
Is the joy that comes back to you.
And the more you spend in blessing
The poor and lonely and sad,
The more of your heart's possessing
Returns to make you glad.

John Greenleaf Whittier (1807–92)

The sun of righteousness

These lines, from Malachi 4:1–6, again look forward to the coming of Christ.
The Saviour is described as one who would bring righteousness and healing.
The prophet Elijah – in New Testament terms, John the Baptist – would be
sent to prepare people for the Lord's coming and to call on them to turn back
to God.

See, the day is coming, burning like an oven, when all the arrogant
and all evildoers will be stubble; the day that comes shall burn them
up, says the LORD of hosts, so that it will leave them neither root nor
branch. But for you who revere my name the sun of righteousness
shall rise, with healing in its wings. You shall go out leaping like calves
from the stall. And you shall tread down the wicked, for they will be
ashes under the soles of your feet, on the day when I act, says the
LORD of hosts.

Remember the teaching of my servant Moses, the statutes and
ordinances that I commanded him at Horeb for all Israel.

Lo, I will send you the prophet Elijah before the great and terrible
day of the LORD comes. He will turn the hearts of parents to their
children and the hearts of children to their parents, so that I will not
come and strike the land with a curse.

Swords into ploughshares

This reading, from Micah 4:1–7, looks forward to an end to war and to a time of lasting peace, and this makes it especially appropriate for the season of goodwill.

In days to come the mountain of the LORD's house shall be established as the highest of the mountains, and shall be raised up above the hills. Peoples shall stream to it, and many nations shall come and say: 'Come, let us go up to the mountain of the LORD, to the house of the God of Jacob; that he may teach us his ways and that we may walk in his paths.' For out of Zion shall go forth instruction, and the word of the LORD from Jerusalem. He shall judge between many peoples, and shall arbitrate between strong nations far away; they shall beat their swords into ploughshares, and their spears into pruning-hooks; nation shall not lift up sword against nation, neither shall they learn war any more; but they shall all sit under their own vines and under their own fig trees, and no one shall make them afraid; for the mouth of the LORD of hosts has spoken.

For all the peoples walk, each in the name of its god, but we will walk in the name of the LORD our God for ever and ever.

On that day, says the LORD, I will assemble the lame and gather those who have been driven away, and those whom I have afflicted. The lame I will make the remnant, and those who were cast off, a strong nation; and the LORD will reign over them in Mount Zion now and for evermore.

Three damsels in the queen's chamber

*In this poem, Algernon Swinburne combines prayers to the Virgin Mary with a
fanciful depiction of the scene of Christ's birth.*

Three damsels in the queen's chamber,
The queen's mouth was most fair;
She spake a word of God's mother
As the combs went in her hair.
Mary that is of might,
Bring us to thy Son's sight.

They held the gold combs out from her,
A span's length off her head;
She sang this song of God's mother
And of her bearing-bed.
Mary most full of grace,
Bring us to thy Son's face.

When she sat at Joseph's hand,
She looked against her side;
And either way from the short silk band
Her girdle was all wried.
Mary that all good may,
Bring us to thy Son's way.

Mary had three women for her bed,
The twain were maidens clean;
The first of them had white and red,
The third had riven green.
Mary that is so sweet,
Bring us to thy Son's feet.

She had three women for her hair,
Two were gloved soft and shod;
The third had feet and fingers bare,
She was the likest God.
Mary that wieldeth land,
Bring us to thy Son's hand.

She had three women for her ease,
The twain were good women:
The first two were the two Maries,
The third was Magdalen.
Mary that perfect is,
Bring us to thy Son's kiss.

Joseph had three workmen in his stall,
To serve him well upon;
The first of them were Peter and Paul,
The third of them was John.
Mary, God's handmaiden,
Bring us to thy Son's ken.

'If your child be none other man's,
But if it be very mine,
The bedstead shall be gold two spans,
The bed foot silver fine.'
Mary that made God mirth,
Bring us to thy Son's birth.

'If the child be some other man's,
And if it be none of mine,
The manger shall be straw two spans,
Betwixen kine and kine.'
Mary that made sin cease,
Bring us to thy Son's peace.

Christ was born upon this wise,
It fell on such a night,
Neither with sounds of psalteries,
Nor with fire for light.
Mary that is God's spouse,
Bring us to thy Son's house.

The star came out upon the east
With a great sound and sweet:
Kings gave gold to make him feast
And myrrh for him to eat.
Mary, of thy sweet mood,
Bring us thy Son's good.

He had two handmaids at his head,
One handmaid at his feet;
The twain of them were fair and red,
The third one was right sweet.
Mary that is most wise,
Bring us to thy Son's eyes. Amen.

Algernon Swinburne (1837–1909)

The three wise men

The story of the visit of the three wise men, as described in Matthew 2:1–12,
forms an essential part of all Christmas nativities and carol services.

In the time of King Herod, after Jesus was born in Bethlehem of Judea,
wise men from the East came to Jerusalem, asking, 'Where is the child
who has been born king of the Jews? For we observed his star at its
rising, and have come to pay him homage.' When King Herod heard
this, he was frightened, and all Jerusalem with him; and calling
together all the chief priests and scribes of the people, he inquired of
them where the Messiah was to be born. They told him, 'In Bethlehem
of Judea; for so it has been written by the prophet: "And you,
Bethlehem, in the land of Judah, are by no means least among the
rulers of Judah; for from you shall come a ruler who is to shepherd my
people Israel."'

Then Herod secretly called for the wise men and learned from
them the exact time when the star had appeared. Then he sent them to
Bethlehem, saying, 'Go and search diligently for the child; and when
you have found him, bring me word so that I may also go and pay him
homage.' When they had heard the king, they set out; and there, ahead
of them, went the star that they had seen at its rising, until it stopped
over the place where the child was. When they saw that the star had
stopped, they were overwhelmed with joy. On entering the house, they
saw the child with Mary his mother; and they knelt down and paid
him homage. Then, opening their treasure-chests, they offered him
gifts of gold, frankincense, and myrrh. And having been warned in a
dream not to return to Herod, they left for their own country by
another road.

The time draws near the birth of Christ

Here Alfred, Lord Tennyson makes the case for celebrating Christ's birth with festive cheer, contrasting the chills of winter outside with the warmth and plenty indoors at this special time of year.

The time draws near the birth of Christ:
The moon is hid; the night is still;
The Christmas bells from hill to hill
Answer each other in the mist.

Four voices of four hamlets round,
From far and near, on mead and moor,
Swell out and fail, as if a door
Were shut between me and the sound:

Each voice four changes on the wind,
That now dilate, and now decrease,
Peace and goodwill, goodwill and peace
Peace and goodwill, to all mankind.

The time admits not flowers or leaves
To deck the banquet. Fiercely flies
The blast of North and East, and ice
Makes daggers at the sharpen'd eaves,

And bristles all the brakes and thorns
To yon hard crescent, as she hangs
Above the wood which grides and clangs
Its leafless ribs and iron horns

Together, in the drifts that pass
To darken on the rolling brine
That breaks the coast. But fetch the wine,
Arrange the board and brim the glass;

Bring in great logs and let them lie,
To make a solid core of heat;
Be cheerful-minded, talk and treat
Of all things ev'n as he were by.

We keep the day. With festal cheer,
With books and music, surely we
Will drink to him, whate'er he be,
And sing the songs he loved to hear.

Alfred, Lord Tennyson (1809–92)

To him was given dominion

This passage, from Daniel 7:13–14, is a prophecy of one like a son of man who would come; he would be given authority, glory and sovereign power. He would rule over the whole earth and his kingdom would never be destroyed. Christians see this as fulfilled in Jesus, whose rule over the whole earth lasts for ever and will never end.

As I watched in the night visions, I saw one like a human being coming with the clouds of heaven. And he came to the Ancient One and was presented before him. To him was given dominion and glory and kingship, that all peoples, nations, and languages should serve him. His dominion is an everlasting dominion that shall not pass away, and his kingship is one that shall never be destroyed.

Tomorrow shall be my dancing day

This is a traditional English carol of unknown origin. Like a number of other carols, it follows the whole of Christ's life from birth to death.

Tomorrow shall be my dancing day;
I would my true love did so chance
To see the legend of my play,
To call my true love to the dance.

Sing O my love, O my love, my love, my love,
This have I done for my true love.

Then was I born of a virgin pure;
Of her I took fleshly substance.
Thus was I knit to man's nature,
To call my true love to the dance.

In a manger laid and wrapped I was,
So very poor; this was my chance,
Betwixt an ox and a silly poor ass,
To call my true love to my dance.

Then afterwards baptized I was;
The Holy Ghost on me did glance,
My Father's voice heard from above
To call my true love to my dance.

Into the desert I was led,
Where I fasted without substance;
The devil bade me make stones my bread,
To have me break my true love's dance.

The Jews on me they made great suit,
And with me made great variance,
Because they loved darkness rather than light,
To call my true love to my dance.

For thirty pence Judas me sold,
His covetousness for to advance:
"Mark whom I kiss, the same do hold!"
The same is he shall lead the dance.

Before Pilate the Jews me brought,
Where Barabbas had deliverance;
They scourged me and set me at nought,
Judged me to die to lead the dance.

Then on the cross hanged I was,
Where a spear my heart did glance;
There issued forth both water and blood,
To call my true love to my dance.

Then down to hell I took my way
For my true love's deliverance,
And rose again on the third day,
Up to my true love and the dance.

Then up to heaven I did ascend,
Where now I dwell in sure substance
On the right hand of God, that man
May come unto the general dance.

Anonymous

Torches

This carol, sung at both Christmas and New Year, is of traditional Galician origin. It became popular after being given a new musical setting by John Joubert (b.1927).

Torches, torches, run with torches
All the way to Bethlehem!
Christ is born and now lies sleeping:
Come and sing your song to him!

Ah, ro-ro, ro-ro, my baby,
Ah, ro-ro, my love, ro-ro;
Sleep you well, my heart's own darling,
While we sing you our ro-ro.

Sing, my friends, and make you merry,
Joy and mirth and joy again;
Lo! he lives, the King of Heaven,
Now and evermore. Amen.

Anonymous, translated by J. B. Trend (1887–1958)

The twelve days of Christmas

*This traditional Christmas song has its origins in an eighteenth-century
Twelfth Night party game, in which each individual singer had to repeat a
long list of items already cited and then add one of his or her own before the
turn passed to the next person, who had to do the same. It is thought that
originally the items in the universally-known version were mostly birds (the
'pear tree' arising from the French* perdrix, *for 'partridge' and the 'gold rings'
from the Scottish 'goldspinks', for 'goldfinches'). The tune to which it is now
sung is relatively recent, dating from around 1909.*

On the first day of Christmas my true love sent to me
A partridge in a pear tree.

On the second day of Christmas my true love sent to me
Two turtle doves
And a partridge in a pear tree.

On the third day of Christmas my true love sent to me
Three French hens,
Two turtle doves
And a partridge in a pear tree.

On the fourth day of Christmas my true love sent to me
Four calling birds,
Three French hens,
Two turtle doves
And a partridge in a pear tree.

On the fifth day of Christmas my true love sent to me
Five gold rings,
Four calling birds,
Three French hens,
Two turtle doves
And a partridge in a pear tree.

On the sixth day of Christmas my true love sent to me
Six geese a laying,
Five gold rings *(etc.)*

On the seventh day of Christmas my true love sent to me
Seven swans a-swimming,
Six geese a laying (*etc.*)

On the eighth day of Christmas my true love sent to me
Eight maids a-milking,
Seven swans a-swimming (*etc.*)

On the ninth day of Christmas my true love sent to me
Nine ladies dancing,
Eight maids a-milking (*etc.*)

On the tenth day of Christmas my true love sent to me
Ten lords a-leaping,
Nine ladies dancing (*etc.*)

On the eleventh day of Christmas my true love sent to me
Eleven pipers piping,
Ten lords a-leaping (*etc.*)

On the twelfth day of Christmas my true love sent to me
Twelve drummers drumming,
Eleven pipers piping (*etc.*)

Anonymous

Unto us a boy

This carol is of German origin and in its original Latin form dates from the fifteenth century.

Unto us a boy is born!
King of all creation,
Came He to a world forlorn,
The Lord of every nation.

Christ from heaven descending low
Comes, on earth a stranger;
Ox and ass their Owner know,
Becradled in the manger.

Herod then with fear was filled:
'A prince,' he said, 'in Jewry!';
All the little boys he killed
At Bethl'em in his fury.

Now may Mary's son, who came
So long ago to love us,
Lead us all with hearts aflame
Unto the joys above us.

Alpha and Omega He!
Let the organ thunder,
While the choir with peals of glee
Doth rend the air asunder.

*Anonymous, translated by Percy Dearmer (1867–1936) and
G. R. Woodward (1848–1934)*

*Words by Percy Dearmer © Oxford University Press 1928.
Reproduced by permission.*

Unto us is born a Son

This carol is of medieval German origin, appearing in the Moosburg
Gradual *(1355–60) and subsequently in the* Piae Cantiones *(1582). It is
known in both its English and Latin forms and may be sung at Christmas and
on the feast of Holy Innocents.*

Unto us is born a Son,
King of choirs supernal;
To this world He deigns to come
Of lords the Lord eternal.

Lo! He lies within a stall
Where cattle fed before Him;
King of heaven and Lord of all,
They know Him and adore Him.

Rage did Herod then impel,
Whom fearful trembling filled;
On the little boys he fell
And every one he killed.

Born of Mary on this day,
By thy grace translate us
To the realm above, we pray,
Where endless joys await us.

Every voice in quire now blend
To hymn our Saviour, Source and End;
In sweet concord sing we so:
Benedicamus Domino.

Anonymous, translated by
G. R. Woodward (1848–1934) and others

A Victorian Christmas

Many features of modern Christmas festivities were introduced during the reign of Queen Victoria. Here the seventeen-year-old Victoria, not yet queen, records in her diary how she spent Christmas Eve 1836, in company with her former governess Lehzen and her pet spaniel Dash, among others.

Saturday, 24 December, 1836
I awoke after 7 and got up at 8. After 9 breakfasted, at a little after 10 we left Kensington with dearest Lehzen, Lady Conroy and – Dashy! and reached Claremont at a quarter to 12. Played and sang. At 2 dearest Lehzen, Victoire and I went out, and came home at 20 minutes past 3. No one was stirring about the gipsy encampment except George, which I was sorry for as I was anxious to know how our poor friends were, after this bitterly cold night. Played and sang. Received from dearest, best Lehzen as a Christmas box two lovely little Dresden China figures, two pair of lovely little chased gold buttons, a small lovely button with an angel's head which she used to wear herself, and a pretty music book; from good Louis a beautiful piece of Persian stuff for an album; and from Victoire and Emily Gardiner a small box worked by themselves. Wrote my journal, went down to arrange mamma's table for her. At 6 we dined. Mr Edmund Byng and Mr Conroy stayed here. Mr Byng is going to stay here a night or two. Very soon after dinner mamma sent for us into the gallery, where all the things were arranged on different tables. From my dear mamma I received a beautiful massive gold buckle in the shape of two serpents; a lovely little delicate gold chain with a turquoise clasp; a lovely coloured sketch of dearest Aunt Louise by Partridge copied from the picture he brought and so like her; 3 beautiful drawings by Munn, one lovely seaview by Purser and one cattle piece by Cooper (all coloured), 3 prints, a book called finden's Tableau, Heath's Picturesque Annual, Ireland; both these are very pretty; Friendship's Offering and the English Annual for 1837, The Holy Land illustrated beautifully, two handkerchiefs, a very pretty black satin apron trimmed with red velvet, and two almanacks. I am very thankful to my dear mamma for all these very pretty things. From dear Uncle Leopold a beautiful turquoise ring; from the Queen a fine piece of Indian gold tissue; and from Sir J. Conroy a print. I gave my dear Lehzen a green morocco jewel case, and the Picturesque Annual; mamma gave her a shawl, a pair of turquoise earrings, an annual, and handkerchiefs. I then took

mamma to the Library where my humble table was arranged; I gave her a bracelet made of my hair, and the Keepsake, and Oriental Annual. Stayed up till eleven.

Princess Victoria (1819–1901)

The Virgin Mary had a baby boy

This is a traditional Trinidadian carol, originally sung by black slaves working on the plantations there in the early nineteenth century. It has become much more widely known since being collected by Edric Connor in 1945 and published in The Edric Connor Collection of West Indian Spirituals and Folk Tunes.

The Virgin Mary had a baby boy,
The Virgin Mary had a baby boy,
The Virgin Mary had a baby boy,
And they say that his name was Jesus.

He come from the glory,
He come from the glorious kingdom:
O yes, believer!
O yes, believer!
He come from the glory,
He come from the glorious kingdom!

The angels sang when the baby born,
The angels sang when the baby born,
The angels sang when the baby born,
And proclaim Him the Saviour Jesus.

The wise men went where the baby born,
The wise men went where the baby born,
The wise men went where the baby born,
And they say that his name was Jesus.

Anonymous

The voice in the wilderness

The words of this passage from Isaiah 40:1–11 describe the preparation for the coming of the Lord, which the New Testament sees as a significant aspect of the life of John the Baptist. Good news is coming, of salvation to all people. This passage is quoted in the oratorio Messiah *(1742) by George Frideric Handel.*

Comfort, O comfort my people, says your God. Speak tenderly to Jerusalem, and cry to her that she has served her term, that her penalty is paid, that she has received from the LORD's hand double for all her sins.

A voice cries out: 'In the wilderness prepare the way of the LORD, make straight in the desert a highway for our God. Every valley shall be lifted up, and every mountain and hill be made low; the uneven ground shall become level, and the rough places a plain. Then the glory of the LORD shall be revealed, and all people shall see it together, for the mouth of the LORD has spoken.'

A voice says, 'Cry out!' And I said, 'What shall I cry?' All people are grass, their constancy is like the flower of the field. The grass withers, the flower fades, when the breath of the Lord blows upon it; surely the people are grass. The grass withers, the flower fades; but the word of our God will stand for ever. Get you up to a high mountain, O Zion, herald of good tidings; lift up your voice with strength, O Jerusalem, herald of good tidings, lift it up, do not fear; say to the cities of Judah, 'Here is your God!' See, the Lord God comes with might, and his arm rules for him; his reward is with him, and his recompense before him. He will feed his flock like a shepherd; he will gather the lambs in his arms, and carry them in his bosom, and gently lead the mother sheep.

Wassail! wassail all over town!

Otherwise known as 'The Gloucestershire wassail', this is a traditional English carol based on the ancient custom of wassailing. This involved groups of singers passing from house to house in a locality, toasting the good luck of their hosts and being rewarded with gifts of food and drink. The term 'wassail' means 'good health!'

Wassail! wassail all over town!
Our toast it is white and our ale it is brown;
Our bowl it is made of the white maple tree:
With the wassailing-bowl we'll drink to thee!

So here is to Cherry and to his right cheek!
Pray God send our master a good piece of beef,
And a good piece of beef that we all may see;
With the wassailing-bowl we'll drink to thee!

And here is to Dobbin and his right eye!
Pray God send our master a good Christmas pie,
And a good Christmas pie that we may all see;
With our wassailing-bowl we'll drink to thee!

So here is to Broad May and to her broad horn!
May God send our master a good crop of corn,
And a good crop of corn that we may all see;
With the wassailing-bowl we'll drink to thee!

And here is to fillpail and to her left ear!
Pray God send our master a happy new year,
And a happy new year as e'er he did see;
With our wassailing-bowl we'll drink to thee!

And here is to Colly and to her long tail!
Pray God send our master he never may fail
A bowl of strong beer; I pray you draw near,
And our jolly wassail it's then you shall hear.

Come, butler, come fill us a bowl of the best,
Then we hope that your soul in heaven may rest;
But if you do draw us a bowl of the small,
Then down shall go butler, bowl and all!

Then here's to the maid in the lily-white smock
Who tripped to the door and slipped back the lock;
Who tripped to the door and pulled back the pin,
For to let these jolly wassailers in.

Anonymous

Watts's cradle hymn

Isaac Watts was the author of over 750 hymns, of which this lullaby is one of the most popular. Though written specifically for children, it is interesting to note that Isaac Watts had no children of his own. Published in 1706, it is sung to a traditional American tune, itself possibly derived from a European folk tune.

Hush! my dear, lie still and slumber;
Holy angels guard thy bed!
Heav'nly blessings without number
Gently falling on thy head.
Sleep, my babe; thy food and raiment,
House and home thy friends provide:
All without thy care or payment,
All thy wants are well supplied.

How much better thou'rt attended
Than the Son of God could be
When from heaven he descended
And became a child like thee!
Soft and easy is thy cradle,
Coarse and hard thy Saviour lay
When his birth-place was a stable
And his softest bed was hay.

Was there nothing but a manger
Cursed sinners could afford
To receive the heav'nly stranger?
Did they thus affront their Lord?
Soft! my child; I did not chide thee,
Though my song might sound too hard:
'Tis thy mother sits beside thee,
And her arms shall be thy guard.

See the kindly shepherds round him,
Telling wonders from the sky!
Where they sought him, there they found him,
With his Virgin Mother nigh.
See the lovely Babe addressing:
Lovely Infant, how he smiled!
When he wept, the mother's blessing
Soothed and hushed the Holy Child.

Lo! he slumbers in his manger,
Where the horned oxen fed;
Peace, my darling, here's no danger,
Here's no ox a-near thy bed.
May'st thou live to know and fear him,
Trust and love him all thy days;
Then go dwell for ever near him,
See his face and sing his praise!

Isaac Watts (1674–1748)

We three kings of Orient are

This popular Epiphany carol was the work of the rector of Christ's Church in Williamsport, Pennsylvania. It was written around 1837 and first published in 1865. It is unusual in attributing particular verses to each of the individual kings.

We three kings of Orient are,
Bearing gifts we traverse afar,
Field and fountain, moor and mountain,
Following yonder star.

O star of wonder, star of night,
Star with royal beauty bright,
Westward leading, still proceeding,
Guide us to thy perfect light.

Gaspard:
Born a king on Bethlehem plain,
Gold I bring to crown him again,
King for ever, ceasing never
Over us all to reign.

Melchior:
Frankincense to offer have I,
Incense owns a Deity nigh;
Prayer and praising all men raising,
Worship him, God on high.

Balthazar:
Myrrh is mine; its bitter perfume
Breathes a life of gathering gloom;
Sorrowing, sighing, bleeding, dying,
Sealed in the stone-cold tomb.

Glorious now behold him arise,
King, and God, and sacrifice.
Heaven sing: 'Alleluia';
'Alleluia' the earth replies.

John Henry Hopkins (1820–91)

We wish you a merry Christmas

This Christmas song has its roots in the wassailing tradition. The origins of the familiar, cheery tune are obscure, though it is sometimes described as an 'old English or Scottish air'.

We wish you a merry Christmas,
We wish you a merry Christmas,
We wish you a merry Christmas,
And a happy new year!

Now bring us some figgy pudding,
Now bring us some figgy pudding,
Now bring us some figgy pudding,
and bring it us here!

O we won't go until we've got some,
No, we won't go until we've got some,
We won't go until we've got some,
So give it us here!

O we all like figgy pudding,
Yes, we all like figgy pudding,
We all like figgy pudding,
So bring it out here!

Anonymous

What child is this?

This carol was written around 1865 and is sung to the tune 'Greensleeves', composed in the late fifteenth century. Its author was an English insurance executive and poet.

What child is this who, laid to rest,
On Mary's lap is sleeping,
Whom angels greet with anthems sweet
While shepherds watch are keeping?
This, this is Christ the King,
Whom shepherds guard and angels sing:
Haste, haste to bring him laud,
The Babe, the Son of Mary!

Why lies he in such mean estate
Where ox and ass are feeding?
Good Christians fear: for sinners here
The silent Word is pleading.
Nail, spear shall pierce him through,
The Cross be borne for me, for you;
Hail! hail the Word made flesh,
The Babe, the Son of Mary!

So bring him incense, gold and myrrh;
Come, peasant, king, to own him!
The King of Kings salvation brings:
Let loving hearts enthrone Him!
Raise, raise the song on high!
The Virgin sings her lullaby.
Joy! joy! for Christ is born,
The Babe, the Son of Mary!

William Chatterton Dix (1837–98)

When the fullness of time had come

The summary of the coming of Christ given at Galatians 4:4–6 is one of the most succinct passages referring to the fact that God became a human being. At the appointed time, Jesus Christ came to set free those who were under the law so that we can be adopted as his children and have all the rights of being his children.

But when the fullness of time had come, God sent his Son, born of a woman, born under the law, in order to redeem those who were under the law, so that we might receive adoption as children. And because you are children, God has sent the Spirit of his Son into our hearts, crying, 'Abba! Father!'

While shepherds watched their flocks by night

This popular Christmas carol was penned by Irish-born Poet Laureate Nahum Tate. It was published in 1700 and did much to influence the change from psalm to hymn singing in English churches. For over 80 years it was, in fact, the only Christmas hymn permitted to be sung in Anglican services.

While shepherds watched their flocks by night,
All seated on the ground,
The angel of the Lord came down,
And glory shone around.

'Fear not,' said he (for mighty dread
Had seized their troubled mind),
'Glad tidings of great joy I bring
To you and all mankind.

'To you in David's town this day
Is born of David's line
A Saviour, who is Christ the Lord;
And this shall be the sign:

'The heavenly Babe you there shall find
To human view displayed,
All meanly wrapped in swathing-bands,
And in a manger laid.'

Thus spake the seraph; and forthwith
Appeared a shining throng
Of angels, praising God, who thus
Addressed their joyful song:

'All glory be to God on high,
And to the world be peace!
Goodwill henceforth from heaven to earth
Begin and never cease!'

Nahum Tate (1652–1715)

White Christmas

Perhaps the most often-heard of modern Christmas songs, 'White Christmas' was written by Irving Berlin in 1942 and played a prominent role in the 1954 film of the same title starring Bing Crosby. Prior to that it had also featured in the film Holiday Inn *(1942). A perennial Christmas favourite, it set a new record for sales of a single song.*

I'm dreaming of a white Christmas
Just like the ones I used to know
Where the treetops glisten
And children listen
To hear sleigh bells in the snow.

I'm dreaming of a white Christmas
With every Christmas card I write
May your days be merry and bright
And may all your Christmases be white.

I'm dreaming of a white Christmas
With every Christmas card I write
May your days be merry and bright
And may all your Christmases be white.

Irving Berlin (1888–1989)

Permission has been sought.

The wise men

G. K. Chesterton loved Christmas, with all its trappings, and wrote numerous pieces on the subject. In this poem he ponders the experience of the three wise men, whose Christmas revelation far exceeded any earthly knowledge they had gleaned until then.

Step softly, under snow or rain,
To find the place where men can pray;
The way is all so very plain
That we may lose the way.

Oh, we have learnt to peer and pore
On tortured puzzles from our youth,
We know all labyrinthine lore,
We are the three wise men of yore,
And we know all things but the truth.

We have gone round and round the hill
And lost the wood among the trees,
And learnt long names for every ill,
And served mad gods, naming still
The furies the Eumenides.

The gods of violence took the veil
Of vision and philosophy,
The Serpent that brought all men bale,
He bites his own accursed tail,
And calls himself Eternity.

Go humbly . . . it has hailed and snowed . . .
With voices low and lanterns lit;
So very simple is the road,
That we may stray from it.

The world grows terrible and white,
And blinding white the breaking day;
We walk bewildered in the light,
For something is too large for sight,
And something much too plain to say.

The Child that was ere worlds begun
(... We need but walk a little way,
We need but see a latch undone ...)
The Child that played with moon and sun
Is playing with a little hay.

The house from which the heavens are fed,
The old strange house that is our own,
Where trick of words are never said,
And Mercy is as plain as bread,
And Honour is as hard as stone.

Go humbly, humble are the skies,
And low and large and fierce the Star;
So very near the Manger lies
That we may travel far.

Hark! Laughter like a lion wakes
To roar to the resounding plain.
And the whole heaven shouts and shakes,
For God Himself is born again,
And we are little children walking
Through the snow and rain.

   G. K. Chesterton (1874–1936)

The Word of life

This simple declaration, from 1 John 1:1–4, asserts that Jesus is both fully God and fully human. He is the living one and the source of life. We may share life with God, so that our joy may be full.

We declare to you what was from the beginning, what we have heard, what we have seen with our eyes, what we have looked at and touched with our hands, concerning the word of life – this life was revealed, and we have seen it and testify to it, and declare to you the eternal life that was with the Father and was revealed to us – we declare to you what we have seen and heard so that you also may have fellowship with us; and truly our fellowship is with the Father and with his Son Jesus Christ. We are writing these things so that our joy may be complete.

Zechariah and Elizabeth

The story of the miraculous birth of a son (John the Baptist) to the aged Zechariah and the barren Elizabeth is related at Luke 1:5–25. The angel Gabriel prophesied to Zechariah that Elizabeth would have a son who would be 'great in the sight of the Lord' and who would prepare the way for the coming of Jesus Christ. Zechariah found this prophecy very difficult to believe and so the angel made him unable to speak. Soon afterward, Elizabeth became pregnant.

In the days of King Herod of Judea, there was a priest named Zechariah, who belonged to the priestly order of Abijah. His wife was a descendant of Aaron, and her name was Elizabeth. Both of them were righteous before God, living blamelessly according to all the commandments and regulations of the Lord. But they had no children, because Elizabeth was barren, and both were getting on in years.

Once when he was serving as priest before God and his section was on duty, he was chosen by lot, according to the custom of the priesthood, to enter the sanctuary of the Lord and offer incense. Now at the time of the incense-offering, the whole assembly of the people was praying outside. Then there appeared to him an angel of the Lord, standing at the right side of the altar of incense. When Zechariah saw him, he was terrified; and fear overwhelmed him. But the angel said to him, 'Do not be afraid, Zechariah, for your prayer has been heard. Your wife Elizabeth will bear you a son, and you will name him John. You will have joy and gladness, and many will rejoice at his birth, for he will be great in the sight of the Lord. He must never drink wine or strong drink; even before his birth he will be filled with the Holy Spirit. He will turn many of the people of Israel to the Lord their God. With the spirit and power of Elijah he will go before him, to turn the hearts of parents to their children, and the disobedient to the wisdom of the righteous, to make ready a people prepared for the Lord.' Zechariah said to the angel, 'How will I know that this is so? For I am an old man, and my wife is getting on in years.' The angel replied, 'I am Gabriel. I stand in the presence of God, and I have been sent to speak to you and to bring you this good news. But now, because you did not believe my words, which will be fulfilled in their time, you will become mute, unable to speak, until the day these things occur.'

Meanwhile, the people were waiting for Zechariah, and wondered at his delay in the sanctuary. When he did come out, he could not speak to them, and they realized that he had seen a vision in the sanctuary. He kept motioning to them and remained unable to speak. When his time of service was ended, he went to his home.

After those days his wife Elizabeth conceived, and for five months she remained in seclusion. She said, 'This is what the Lord has done for me when he looked favourably on me and took away the disgrace I have endured among my people.'

Zechariah's song of thanksgiving

This passage, from Luke 1:67–79, is known as the Benedictus ('Praise be') from the opening word in the Latin translation. Here, Zechariah praises God for the provision of salvation for his people and he looks forward to the life and work of John the Baptist who would prepare the way for the Messiah.

Then his father Zechariah was filled with the Holy Spirit and spoke this prophecy:

'Blessed be the Lord God of Israel, for he has looked favourably on his people and redeemed them. He has raised up a mighty saviour for us in the house of his servant David, as he spoke through the mouth of his holy prophets from of old, that we would be saved from our enemies and from the hand of all who hate us. Thus he has shown the mercy promised to our ancestors, and has remembered his holy covenant, the oath that he swore to our ancestor Abraham, to grant us that we, being rescued from the hands of our enemies, might serve him without fear, in holiness and righteousness before him all our days. And you, child, will be called the prophet of the Most High; for you will go before the Lord to prepare his ways, to give knowledge of salvation to his people by the forgiveness of their sins. By the tender mercy of our God, the dawn from on high will break upon us, to give light to those who sit in darkness and in the shadow of death, to guide our feet into the way of peace.'

The child grew and became strong in spirit, and he was in the wilderness until the day he appeared publicly to Israel.